T0064504

ACCEPTANCE

IS THE BEGINNING OF CHANGE

Motivational and Inspirational Memoir

RALSTON G. BISHOP

iUniverse®

DEDICATION

As a token of my appreciation for her love and life,
I dedicate this book to Tameka Williams.

To my beloved sister, gone but not forgotten. If there were ever a time that I wish to switch places with someone, it would have to be the time of my sister passing. My memories of her will prolong and my love for her will never diminish.

Thank you Tameka

APPRECIATION

Thanks to the Almighty God who has blessed me with wisdom, knowledge and strength. A special thanks to the lady of my life, Ava for giving me the well needed support and understanding to complete this book.

I thank all those whom have encouraged me especially, Dr. L. Francis, Brad, Clayton, Terrence, Tamara, Tosanna, and Pastor J. Hemmings. Thanks to Barbara and Lois for providing me with careful analyzed insight. Last but not least, I thank my mother Janet for loving me and raising me, the best way she knew how and even in death she remains a source of inspiration in my life.

Member of
Jamaican Copyright Licensing Agency
17 Ruthven Road, Building 3
Kingston 10, Jamaica
www.jamcopy.com

CONTENTS

INTRODUCTION

It's Easter! Good Friday to be exact and I was watching a movie about Jesus crucifixion on my television broadcasting from one of our local channels. This movie always stirs up my thoughts in many ways. Most significantly, Being reminded of my own trial and temptations, it was then a thought came to my mind, it felt like a burning desire that I had for many years, this desire was to write a book recapping my life. I previously read a book entitled, Barack Obama, *Dreams from My Father*, it is a reflection on Obama's early years before he became President of the United States of America. I admire the way in which Obama try to recapture his early years even his childhood. I reflected for a while on the book and somewhere between the movie and the book, I was prompted to share my own story. Today is not just the recapping of my life but it is a review of my faith and thorough evaluation of who I am arising from actual events.

Let anyone whom had done no wrong
judge me and cast the first stone.

Now to all those who had read or listened to my poems, you would be asking yourself, is there more that I can say about myself that I have not already through poems? However, I want to assure you this, surprise is the very essence of this book, and while suspense is at the very center, pain and pleasure are in every chapter, but truth is in every written word. I invite you to speculate where no names mentioned, because of the nature of this book many would rather not identified personally.

For years, I have tried to block out sections of my life but I had come to full knowledge and acceptance that who I am today is the product of my own successes and failures coupled with God's mercy and grace.

I am encouraged by many of my friends to share my life story however; I found it difficult to write on actual events because my life's journey is a very colorful one. Therefore, even as I contemplate on writing this book, I give great consideration on the repercussions it may cause on my existing life. **But acceptance is the beginning of change**. Unless we are willing to accept that, what we had done or what we are doing is wrong we will never seek to change. This is why acceptance has formed the basis for parole eligibility, for accepting the blame comes with its fair share of consequences; however, I firmly believe it is the right thing to do.

My conscience is my guide so I will set my conscience free so I can be free. I must admit that I am not the type that is good on giving details on any particular event but there is an old-time proverb, "the one who shit into the bushes does not remember it, instead it is remembered by the one who stepped in it." If I were to interpret that proverb, it would simply be that we are more mindful of things when they affect us. You will find that this proverb has a diverse effect and it is very evident in these chapters. I recall one of my uncles saying to me, "Rally I do not know how you do it but I could not have dealt with so much problem and still be alive." (Rally is short for Ralston). I have no doubt that everyone has their fair share of problems but I can only speak of my own problems and my will to overcome. From rags to riches and from riches to rags could easily be the tag line for my life, however, looking on me today I doubt it is a product that you would want to buy. This calls to mind another old-time proverb that could help to define my life, "no one sees you when you are on your way to visit the doctor but everyone sees you when you are coming back." If I may, I will try to simplify this proverb, people will partake in your glory but not your problems. I cannot say this is entirely true because there were many who stood beside me during my tribulations and to all those who did, I say a special thanks.

I know I will write about my mother who played the most valuable part in my life. Neither will I hesitate to write about the lady of my life because she had contributed tremendously to my success. There are actual events that remain on the forefront of my mind that will find their way through these pages although I ask for your forgiveness if I fail to give full details of any such events. I also ask that you not surprised by the events or the many names that I may mention. Furthermore, I ask that you do not ponder on the events or names that you think should mentioned. There is a time and place for everything; this may not be the time and place for what you think is missing. I will try to ease your discontent by saying; some of the details of these events may have a repercussion on my life so bear with me if I withhold them.

I relish the belief that "faith without work is dead" however, my tribulations out weight my faith and hope seems like a distance away. Through it all, I have a story to tell even though the battle has not yet won.

I invite you to crave for these chapters as the feast is good and the benefits are undoubtedly satisfying and fulfilling.

CHAPTER ONE

A baby I came

It was on 19 November 1974 that I first saw the light; my eyes were open to a new world, one that would fill me with knowledge and experiences beyond measure. Please allow me to close my eyes and look on when it all started. I am the fourth child for my mother, her second and last son, and second man-child for my father. It all began in a little District called Parry Town situated above Ocho Rios in the Parish of Saint Ann. It was there my father met my mother; the bond that they shared may be questionable as they never truly shared a home and love never seemed to be present in any discussions. Still they had achieved two sons together, Junior (my older brother) and Ralston (me). Junior being the oldest was also my father first born; he enjoyed the benefits of both parents while growing up. There could be absolutely no doubt about the passion that existed between my mother and father because my brother is one year and a few months older than I am. In fact, it was only another twenty months that I came rushing out of my mother's womb. For what it is worth, the question still lingers in my mind, did my father truly loved my mother? It is among the questions that I never asked, so it is an answer that I never got, even though it remains a concern because of the many different stories that my mother had told me about her relationship with my father, some of which I am a living testimony.

My first encounter with my father was an unforgettable moment. I was about five years of age when I realized that my brother would leave the house Sunday to visit his father (our father). Later he would return with goodies which would include money but none of which I was able to partake, simply because my mother would not allow it. So I decided to accompany my brother this particular Sunday when he went to visit our father. When we got into the house, his wife was home alone and she invited me in because my brother was no stranger. I went in and sat on a chair as she entertained me until he arrived home. As he entered the house and saw me he said, "What are you doing here?" The tone of his question and the manner in which he said it had me running. I ran straight through the door and went home never to return to that house. I understand why through my mother's very short stories, which she often told with a sense of bitterness and hatred for my father. She often took me back to her younger life, recalling the early stages of her pregnancy with me. As she talked about those memories, I could see her humble expression and knowing my mother asking any questions as to why I could not part-take would not have gone down well with her. She began, "It was on a Sunday night, I was on my way home from a movie at the theater in the community, and while walking home I was approached by your father who wanted to know where I was coming from. He asked with strong tone, "Where are you coming from at this hour of the night." She replied to him, "I went about my own business." As my father held unto her hand to prove his strength in an effort to get her full attention, she resisted then reached for a rock that she could hold in her hand and hit him in the head and went on home. Not pleased with what my mother did, my father did not attempt to have another such confrontation with my mother again. As for my mother her hostility and bitterness towards my father seems to be the result of a broken heart. But it is clear to me that they had an unresolved issue, whatever it was; there goes my father leaving my mother with a one-year-old son and an unborn child. After the battle line was drawn the only communication between my mother and father would be about my older brother, who was very sickly as a child. Then I came in the midst of all their controversy, with no father to call my own because he was long gone and a mother too filled with pride to let him own up to his responsibility. I must say thanks to my grandfather Marshall, who stood up to my mother and insisted that she give me my father's surname after she had given birth to me. This was among the many stories my mother told me as a child even as she recalls his words, "If the child is not for Roderick (my father), he is for Balin (my uncle) or he is mine, but he is a Bishop." Hence I was given my birthright, the surname Bishop. Therefore, she decided to raise me on her own despite her many struggles and hardships. I never have to speak to my father until I was about seventeen during the time of my graduation. I want to share with you that brief moment and beyond as I fast track some of the years. It was the time of my graduation, I was short on cash, and I was encouraged by my brother to ask my father for money for my graduation. I was shy and afraid at first to confront him, but as soon as I saw him, he greeted me as his son and that removed my fear. I remember the day like it was yesterday, he was at the Almond Tree Restaurant and Bar doing his construction work he was a building contractor. I walked towards him and before I could make any utterance, he greeted me as his son. From that day forward, we enjoyed a good relationship. However, as the relationship progressed, I sought answers as to why he did not own me as his son during my earlier years. His response was he could not afford the both of us, (meaning my brother and I) so he chose one over the other. That for me was never a good answer but I had already forgiven him and moved on with my life.

I have no doubt in my mind my mother loved me with an exceptional love, and if I may be so bold, she loved me from birth. As I recall, my mother told me that it was on a Thursday afternoon she was home doing her daily chores when she felt a liquid substance running down her legs, her water had broken making way for the unborn child that was inside her. She must have thought to herself, there is no time to get to a hospital, because the nearest hospital was over seven miles away, in Saint Ann's Bay, and with limited transportation that hardly seemed an option. So she did the next best thing, she asked someone to call for Nurse Allen who lived just about half mile away. I can imagine the look on my mother's face, filled with anguish and unbearable pain and I can imagine the strong anticipation of my grandmother (Sissy Lyn) and all those who linger around to greet the new born. As she anxiously waited to push out the unborn child, whom was just as equally eager to get out, they were all there to ensure the bed linens were clean while rendering some level of comfort to my mother although no one could help her deal with the pain. They had informed the nurse and she was on her way rushing to assist my mother in her delivery of the unborn child. I could easily paint a picture of Nurse Allen, repeating in her mind, "I can do this; this is what I was trained for." This was her first practical experience in delivering a child, so you can now imagine her nervousness. So she was finding courage in her training, as my mother positioned herself to give birth to the child. For my mother it was familiar territory as this was her fourth child, for her it was routine but the pain could not tamed. The bed linen was clean, my mother held her position and do not even ask, if I held my position because I was more than ready to get out there. The nurse instructed my mother to push. Her heart was beating wildly as the nurse uttered repeatedly. Push! Push! There is the head, push! There is a shoulder, push! The nurse smiled and breathes a sigh of relief it's a "boy." My mother might have said, "Thank God that was over." Not knowing this was only the beginning of her pain.

Winsome Walker, my mother's closest friend at the time, was also eagerly anticipating my birth and had already prepared a name for me. This was also among my mother's short stories. Ralston McKenzie was the host of a program on the radio called "Sunday Connection" and this program tried to unite lost relatives and families. Winsome loved that program and would listen frequently to it. She suggested naming me after this radio host, my mother accepted, and hence I got the name Ralston. Not much was mentioned of my middle name (Garth) so I am assuming it must have been a name my mother had stumbled across and thought it would be perfect for me and it worked, because I am often told that I have a perfect name and the truth is I love my name.

> "so as a babe I came, so she gave me a name, milk I
> would get as I lay on my mother's chest to feed from her
> breast, as I cry she give me more just to make sure, my
> bones were strong in her eyes I could do no wrong."
> Quote from my poem entitled "My Mother"

CHAPTER TWO

Then I grew

"A single parent I knew as I grew, she did not own a house but in a home I grew. She did it with pride and God by her side. She taught me equity, respect and never to forget, to be thankful and not boastful."
Quote from my poem entitled "My Mother"

This is my view; I firmly believe it is hard for a single parent to raise a child effectively, especially when that single parent can hardly provide for the home. From my own personal experiences and encounters that I had with known criminals, most children who turn to crime or become violent are from a single parent homes. I say this because I am a living testimony to that belief. Because of my mother inability to provide for her home, out of love I felt compelled to share her burden. This compelling force literally turns me into a hunter and provider by any means necessary but I had my own fair share of challenges even while seeking to do that, which was good. Growing up with a single parent is never an easy life and if that was not enough, I had a brother who, although he was older he needed more attention because of his childhood illness. I fell in the center of my mother's seven children, Carolyn, Tracy-Ann, Junior, Ralston, Tamara, Tameka and Tosanna. I never knew Carolyn because she died before I was born. I cannot take away the fact that I am the fourth child but I was never the center of attraction except when I am needed to bridge the gap or to fix something that is broken, whether it be physically, socially or emotionally. For that, I am always the intermediary, picking up the pieces and making sure the family taken care of, by making the necessary sacrifices. So right then and there the youngest became the oldest or as some would say, "the boy became the man." I must admit though, there were times when I became jealous over my brother knowing that he had a mother and father and all I had is a mother with whom I had to share. I always called him the lucky one. However, as the years went by I realized he needed it much more.

I am bless with a strong will, a sense of determination and self-motivated ambition. This I learned at a very tender age, although it took some time for it to groom properly, as I was often misguided. In the earlier years of my childhood I grew up in a happy home, I may not have had the best of meals but I had love. Surrounded by my grandmother Sissy Lyn, who later passed away when I was eight years old, my mother, sisters and brother, my uncle Keith and his immediate family; we lived in a big house for a big family but all of that was about to change. Uncle Keith decided that he wanted the house all for himself. After the death of my grandmother, my mother and we children were remove from the house. That big house was the only house we had known.

The "hunter" is what I was call, and if I might add, I was very quick with my fingers and age was not any significance in this matter. By the time, I realized that I could run around the house, I was outside and into the bushes hunting for fruits, with my favorites being the mangoes, apples, oranges, ripe bananas, oh! What am I saying? I love them all, "if you say fruits you say Ralston or you know where to find me." I have such a great love for fruits, there were moments when I could easily sense where to go and find the next fruit tree that was ready for harvest even if it was on the neighbor's property. However, there was one thing for sure, I dare not take any home for my mother to see or else she would send me back from whence I came with a proper beating, so I could only pick what could hold in my pockets and my stomach.

> "Did I tell you that I was bad, so she did not spare the
> rod, because she was ashamed and sad, so across my
> back she would stretch her strap, so that I would stop?"
> Quote from my poem entitled "My Mother"

I always had cravings for ripe bananas, and my neighbor, Miss Daphne would pay dearly to satisfy that appetite. She owned the property situated in front of the house that I grew up in and on that property, there were plenty of banana trees, or should I say enough for me to reap. She did not visit her property frequently so it gave me a clear opportunity to keep watch until they were ripe and ready to reap. It was very easy to know when Miss Daphne was on her property, so there was no fear of being exposed. Usually as she entered her property, she starts complaining to herself but it was direct to anyone who would steal her things including me. She was never short on words that sometimes cut like a razor and her favorite line was "the old living dead them that won't leave my things" for me that was neither here nor there but it would prompt my mother to send a strong warning out, "Ralston! I hope you did not trouble Miss Daphne things, or else!" I quickly replied with a sweet innocent voice, "No Mama it wasn't me." Somehow, my mother always had a way of seeing way beyond that innocent look on my face, she could see right through me.

I must admit, I was not among what you would call the average child, who would want a toy for Christmas or maybe it was because I could see right through my mother's financial status and already knew that she could not afford it. Therefore, I did not set my desires in that direction, but I do remember making my own toys from the juice boxes and bottle corks. I would create toy trucks and cars that I would play with in the street of our home, occasionally with my brother or any company as being alone was never an issue for me. I have always enjoyed my own company from as far back as I can remember. However, playing in the street did not come without its own challenges. I remember playing with my homemade toys in the middle of the street while my brother played with his toys below me. I then felt the presence of someone or something. I raised my head to see what it was, as I look up I saw a man stepping towards me. I then turn to my brother and said, "Watch out a man is coming!" He looked at me and asked, "Which man?" I look back around and the next thing I know I am running. My brother told the record of what happen from that point on, which was often to mock or for his own amusement. My brother found that amusing because he never saw the man that I was trying to show him. My brother would often say, "I saw you run from the street and fall on the veranda, you began kicking your feet, and foam was coming from your mouth. Then mama picked you up and took you to Paw (Paw was the known village Obeah man). "He gave you three grains of white rice and some sweet sugar and water and then read a book over you." As for my mother, she was concerned as to what happened and she told me Paw's interpretation of what might happened to me. Paw said, "He saw a ghost that was going about its own way. When the boy stared at it, he was not strong enough to stand up to it. So it over powered him and that is why he ran and fainted." There was no three grains of rice and any sugar and water mentioned in my mother's version of the story, but my brother was holding on to his version. I guess it was more entertaining but whatever it was, since that day I never had any such fainting again, although I still see things no one else sees.

I can easily say I had my fair share of laughter when it comes to my brother, because he was always afraid of just about any and everything that moved in the dark. He was easily frightened but despite that, he would still stay out late to collect his own supply from the bakery in the community that ran a late night shift. One late night my mother had decided to give him a scare as a means of punishment for staying out late. She wrapped herself with a white cotton sheet and waited outside for him to arrive. When he arrived, she walked towards him making scary sounds. As soon as my brother heard and saw something he could not identify, he tossed all the patties he had in his hand at my mother and began swearing and cursing while beating on the door begging for someone to let him inside the house. We were all too busy enjoying the entertainment as the house filled with laughter. By the time, my grandmother decided to let him in, he was almost breathless and tears were running down his face. In addition, we laughed even more. That did stop my brother from staying out late at night and other occasions when he would come home bawling, swearing, cursing and beating on the door. Those days where packed with fun and mischief.

I remember my preschool teachers although there is not much that stands out about them except for their names, Miss Nanny and Miss Mitzie. Miss Nanny, I used to find her name to be funny and Miss Mitzie was a tongue twister for me, but maybe it was a result of my heavy tongue. There were times when others would ask me to say words that would be hard for me pronounce just so someone could get a laugh, but that seems to be outdated now, my tongue is much lighter and I speak more fluently. I somehow blessed with a tag team while going through preschool, one of my younger sisters, Tamara. Tamara would cry every morning as I was about ready to leave for school until my mother decided that she would attend school with me and then the tears stopped flowing. She has to enter preschool when she was just about two years of age; all of this was just so she could be around me all day. My mother handed down this recollection of memory.

As I said, my childhood days were fun and mischievous. Although I was not much of a swimmer then, I loved to go by the river. The truth is the only time I would enter the water is when my brother and cousins were on the other side of the bank. I had a fear of them throwing me out in the deep; they made numerous attempts but were unsuccessful because I was also quick on my feet. I would ran away because I did not find their way of teaching me to swim amusing and the truth is I found it detrimental, so it was catch me if you can and I managed to learn how to swim on my own.

Unfortunately, I have a very brief memory of my mother's parents, although I grew up knowing them but still the memories of them seem to be fading by the years. My grandmother was the closest to my heart as we shared more together owing to the fact that I grew up in her house while she was still alive. What I remember most about her was she would always ensure that every Sunday we had to attend church. She was always kind and caring, willing to share her every meal even if it was just a piece of orange or her favorite whole-wheat biscuits. My oldest sister was her favorite grandchild so most of the time we would only get what Tracy did not want. My grandmother would stand up as my savior when my mother had decided to give me a beating for something that I had done wrong. I can still remember her saying to my mother, "Leave the boy alone." Then my mother would put away the whip. Underneath her bed was a safe haven for me when my mother would try to catch me.

On the other hand, my grandfather Richard (Mas Dick) lived about a mile away from where we lived, quiet, simple, peaceful, sharing, humble, these are some of the words that were used to describe my grandfather, but he was always firm on his decisions. The one thing I remember most about my grandfather is a haircut he gave me; I called it the haircut of my life. It all happened on a day after I was making my regular visit to his house; he was his usual observant self as he saw that I had caught lice. He sat me down underneath a mango tree that was in his backyard; he then took out his pair of scissors and razor and began to trim away with the scissors as he prepared my head for shaving. Not long after the razor came into play, he scraped my head until I could not feel a single hair. Then he roasted a very sour orange and he rubbed it all over my head. From that day forward, wherever there are lice I stay away because I never wanted to have my hair trimmed like that again. Nevertheless, I thanked him for a job well done because I was free from the nagging bites I was getting from their blood sucking mouths. I do not wish to take value from the previous story you just read. I can recall similar haircut story when I was seven year old. I was sent to my granduncle, Uncle Clement, whose hands were shaking like a small tree on a windy day and by the time he was finished I end up with the worst hair cut ever, I had to hide my head for days, just waiting for it grow back. I found myself working twice as hard, to avoid getting that haircut again.

My grandfather was never big on cooking but most of time something was always there to eat. He had some fried chicken in the basket, tasting like it came from one of the famous fast-food restaurants. The fried chicken was always lock away in a plastic container, placed in a basket and tied to the ceiling for safekeeping. With the fried chicken was some freshly cooked white rice. My grandfather was a farmer so you could always look forward to some food from the farm, "ground provisions" as they would have called it. Some freshly made coconut oil added to that made it a delightful meal. That may not sound like much to you, but to me that was more than enough, I ate it while licking my fingers. When I was ready to leave, I was focus on the ripe bananas and the pocket change I would get when I am leaving. I remember we visited my grandfather, that is my brother and I, and when it was about time to leave, he gave us a large box filled with ripe bananas to take for our mother and some pocket change for ourselves. We had to walk back home, which was customary in those days because there was limited means of transportation. Therefore, we were partners in carrying the box, on our way home we stopped at the first nearby shop and bought some bullas and two drinks of "suck-suck". At about a quarter of the journey, we stopped again, but only this time we were going to have a feast and so we did. We ate approximately half of the bananas, drank all the drinks and ate all the bullas. We were *stuffed*. You easily smelled ripe bananas coming from our breath. There was no telling of truth since no question asked. My mother only found out a week later after she had visited my grandfather, and then came the beating. There were times when we had to walk over three miles to visit our grandfather's field to help him harvest his crops, but who was measuring the distance, for us in those days, it was all day of fun or it was like being on a field trip where we would get to stop by the river.

Talking about the good-old -days may seem like a myth or just a thing of the past, but for me it is as real today and it is what helped me appreciate the strength and determination of my family. Whether it be the hovering and spiritual discipline from my grandmother or the kindness blended with firm discipline from my grandfather, it was all good for growth and development and would eventually become useful at some point in life, for though the journey maybe long and the battle maybe hard, as a family we withstood the test and stand firm.

CHAPTER THREE

I was bad

"Did I tell you how I was bad, so she did not spear
the rod, because she was ashamed and sad, so across
my back she would stretch her strap so that I would
stop?" Quote from my poem entitled "My Mother"

Growing up poor has its fair share of challenges and I can give testimonies
to that. My clothing was not always the best and my cologne was the scent
of green Cedar tree. My meals were not always something to brag about
except for those special Sundays or special provisions. I must admit I never
easily accept gifts and I seldom ate what offered to me. It was a hard task
for someone who would want to offer me a meal, because I would boldly
refuse.

My school days became harder as I finished Basic School. In fact, going
through Primary School is when I felt the real pinch of poverty and school
was a must, even if I tried to hide or fuss. For lunch my mother would
provide us with homemade baked products often times cornmeal pudding
or blue draws and enough money to buy something to drink when it was
available. My oldest sister, Tracy would safeguard everything because my
mother feared we (my brother and I) would partake of it before our lunch
break. However, for us that was an up-hill task because Tracy's class always
seemed to be the last to take lunch breaks. When I could no longer hold
in the hunger, I went in search for anything the other students refused so
I could have something to eat. Those were embarrassing moments. So I
upped my game and resorted to stealing. Although this is never something

to brag about, I had needs and desires that needed fulfilling. As I grew those needs and desires grew within me. I can truly say without exception poverty breeds crime.

I was about nine years of age; it was on a quiet Thursday morning no school was in session. I was walking home after doing some errands for my mother with one final stop to make. I had some pocket change, so I stopped at a nearby shop to buy myself some candy. As I entered the shop, I observed that there was no shopkeeper, so I began calling out for some assistance. "Serve! Serve!" No one answered. "Serve! Serve!" Still no one answered. I began observing the settings of the shop to see what was available, as I looked around I saw a transparent bag hanging from the shelves with money inside of it. I immediately checked my surrounding to see if there was anyone watching and by this time the purchase of candy was no longer on my mind, it was now the bag with the money. I swiftly reached around the counter, grabbed the bag of money, and quickly made my way out of the shop. I remembered I still have one more stop to make which was to check for mail at the post office. I was comforted by the fact that I did not see or hear anyone and with the money now hidden away in my underwear it was safe for me to stop by the post office or at least that is what I thought. By the time I got to the post office and asked for the mail, I heard a voice shout, "See him deh." (There he is). Before I could turn around to see who it was, a boy much older than I am grabbed me in the back of my shirt and said, "I just saw him leaving the shop." A woman who was in no laughing mood then confronted me; she started her line of interrogation, "Where is the money boy?" I nervously replied. "What money are you talking?" As I began to plead my innocence, she began searching my pockets but came up empty. "Where is the money boy?" She asked again. As I was about to continue to plead my innocence, she raised her hand and slapped me across my face and I was not about to wait for another. By this time my nervousness became fear, I quickly reached for the money that was in my underwear, pushed it into her hand, and made a run for it. I must have called on the strength of ten tigers like the Phantom because I had found an unthinkable strength that allowed me to free myself from the boy who was holding my shirt. I am not an athlete but I believe that the fastest man alive could not have caught me that day! I ran straight home and when I walked in my mother called, "Ralston?"

"Yes Mama!"

"Did you get any letter from the post office?"

"No Mama." I answered while breathing a sigh of relief knowing that the news had not reached her ears, at least not yet. The evening came swiftly and I was soon to get another call from my mother. By this time, the news had started to spread throughout the community how I was exposed trying to steal from the shop. "Ralston come here!" My mother called with a calm voice. As I walked towards her, she took hold of my hand firmly, my instinct telling me something was wrong. She began asking question about what had happened earlier in the day. Now I knew something was wrong, so the tears immediately started to flow. "Why did you go into the shop and steal the shopkeeper's money?" She asked. While no word was forth coming from my mouth, the beating was ready and already prepared, so she did not hesitate for a second. That day she whipped me with pride, anger and disappointment. I tell you that she used both hands with equal amount of accuracy and strength. As one hand got tired, it was time for the next to come in on the action. She whipped me that day until I could no longer cry because there was no sound coming from my mouth but my brother had picked up where I had left off and he did cry. He cried as if he was feeling every blow, I could see him with his hands on his head and tears running down on his face. He was shouting with a very loud voice, "Murder! Murder!" He cried repeatedly and although no one would respond to my cry for help, it was rather impossible to ignore my brother's cry of murder. The neighbors gathered round with a plea to my mother to stop the beating because there was no grandmother around to save me that day. But no one would go near her because she was like a raving bull, so my mother gave me the full extent of her wrath and as she came toward the end of her whipping I can still remember hearing her breathing heavily as she utter these words, "A shame you want shame me boy!" I will never forget those words even though I heard them in much pain and by the time she was finished whipping me I was swollen all over my body. I thank God she never had to beat me like that again. The truth is my mother never was one who put up with my wrong doings, however, that never stopped me from stealing. What I did receive from that beating, made me smarter by not allowing myself to be caught or more importantly, being able to conceal things from my mother so that she would not feel ashamed of me again. I went on stealing. It became a bad habit, it had taken a hold of me, and even when I was not in need, I would steal just to satisfy the needs of others.

I recall a particular incident while I was "looking my food" still young and inexperienced I would take just about anything that would present itself as an easy take. As usual, I watched this house and studied the movements of the occupant but I miscalculated this time. When I decided to make my move, I went by the window, which was a louver glass window and proceeded to remove the blades to gain entrance to the house. As I entered the house, I saw a boy much younger than I was sleeping. I forgot to tell you it was night. I hesitated for a while but only for a while. That did not prevent me from making a thorough search of the house before I left and I did not need any pigeon powder to keep the boy still sleeping. So I quietly make my search of the house and after I found my loot, I discretely exited the way I entered leaving the little boy sleeping in his bed. This added to my level of determination and confidence, if I really wanted something. This time I headed in the wrong direction and it would not stop there. I stepped up my game as I grow in age and knowledge, devising my own plans and executing them successfully even as I moved onto greater challenges that came with greater risk. Having a strong determination and being very articulate, I had a gift to command or influence others; I could easily pull off any job once I saw the just cause and in doing so, leaving no trace behind. Regretfully, time or my own actions would expose me in very short order. I remember in brief, the Principal of the Primary School that I was attending, placed me in a dark room for detention. I was in the fourth grade in an overcrowded classroom, with most of the children who could not afford to buy their own lunch. Therefore, I decided on my own that I was going to feed a few of them. After I had carefully observed the operations of the cafeteria, I planned my move and buying was not a part of that plan. I waited until the classes where in session, the cafeteria was vacant, and I put my plan in action. I took all that could hold in my bag and made a clean escape. I went back to my classroom and gave away all the food and drinks to my classmates and those who were in need did not bother to ask from whence it came, they ate gladly. The following day the Principal sent me for and as I entered his office, I saw one of the students from my classroom. He had gotten caught stealing food and drinks from the cafeteria and he was making a plea bargain. Therefore, I became the scapegoat and I had very little defense because even those whom enjoyed yesterday's feast where willing to testify against me. The Principal described me as the mastermind behind the stealing so you can easily guess what happened after that or allow me to cut a long story short, I was locked up in the detention room. By the way, I did escape from the detention room, after I managed to force open the window blades that were metal; I hastily made my way through. I would later hide myself for days from school until the smoke cleared and without my mother gaining any knowledge of what was going on. I easily recall the days when my lunches were free or at the expense of the vendors. I would stand by and watch until their stalls were crowded and then I would make my move as if I was a paying customer. If my cover blown I would quickly ask for my change as if I had paid. Those days the lunch was never too expensive for me because I did not care about the price since paying was not my first option. An interesting observation is, even at that tender age, I chose whom I stole from at all times. If a stall did not seem to be in good order and filled with plenty of goods, I would not take from it; in fact, I looked for those that were flourishing for me to steal from them.

There were times when I sat down and asked myself the question, "When did I become a thief?" The answer would always come to me with more questions. Questions like, "Did it all begin at the shop? Was it Miss Icy's apples? Before she woke up in the morning or late at night, I would pick her apples. Was it Captain's mangoes? The ones that were located beside his house but still I would skillfully pick them without leaving a trace or was it Miss Daphne's ripe bananas? That I would timely watch and patiently reap despite the warnings and the name-calling." Devious and skillful I was indeed. The biggest question was "is this right" or is this who I want to be?" My mother disapproved so she was always in the dark and life would soon disapprove and place me in the dark. It was hard for me to say where it all began; I can truly say I got better and better over the years. However, I knew it all had to end one day and what greater day there is than today.

From one bad habit came another, the habit of gambling was now a part of my life. Stealing and gambling are the two worst habits any man could have with exception of alcohol and drug addiction but I was never much of a drinker or smoker although I would soon have my share. Regardless, the gambling took a hold of me, I would play anything that came with a bet, and if I did not know the game, I was willing to learn even though the price was very costly at times. I began dealing the cards from as far back as Primary School right through High School at any and every given break. I was always ready for a good game, I quickly moved on to master the game of dominoes, which comes with its fair share of wins and losses. However, I found checkers to be more fun. I could never ignore a poker box, and once it was on, I would purchase change to play. But it was at a tremendous loss most of the time, so it did not take me long to learn that I should stay away from gambling, yet the stealing stuck around a little longer.

As I grew up leaving my teenage years behind, I left my mother's house and went to live with my Granduncle Clement. We shared a history and it was a transformation period in my life and a chapter of new beginnings. It was a time when I began to realize what it took to be a man and it was a time when the girls started rushing in. But it was more than just that, it was a time when I get to care for an elderly man who was in need of care. During my time living with my granduncle, I watched him grow weaker and weaker as he grew older. While he was strong, I learned much from his simple and kind ways until he fell ill and could no longer move around the house. He survived two mild strokes in two years before he passed on. During his illness, he was bedridden and was unable to feed himself, so I had to ensure he had his meals on time and his daily bath. I also had to kept clean his bed linen and clothes even if I had to do the laundry myself, which I often did. Overall, he was a good teacher but I was not a good student or I was just too slow. He could identify a woman of good character from a mile off and he would often point it out to me, but would I listen? No! Too young and too slow to learn so I would soon learn the hard way. It was during this same time I had my first bad experience with the law that landed me in jail.

Approximately January in the year 1996, I was in my early twenties and had just started working at the Jamaica Grande Beach Resort. I went to an ATM to make a withdrawal with my card; I put my card inside the ATM not knowing that I did not have enough money in the bank. It showed up on the screen that I did not have enough cash to continue with the transaction, so I removed my card and stepped outside of the ATM room. While standing outside with no cash contemplating my journey home after a long night of work, I thought of the distance that I have to walk in order to reach home. Something got into my thoughts telling me that I should try the ATM again. So I went back in only this time I did not intend to use an ATM card. I covered my face with my handkerchief and got to work by trying from every possible angle to open the ATM but my efforts proven futile. So I got out, walked straight home felling tired and broke. A few days later, I saw a police jeep parked at my gate and two police officers got out of the jeep. They were courteous as they asked my name, I identified myself and they asked if they could come inside. Not knowing what they were about, I did not hesitate to invite them in. They introduced themselves as Constable E and Constable S then they began explaining to me why they came to see me. They explained that a woman had come by the station and lodged a complaint against you, claiming that you stole some clothing from her and we want to verify her allegations. The officers continued by asking if they could have a look at my clothing to see if any of them match the description of that of the woman's. I allowed them free access as they searched through my clothes piece by piece. My granduncle was his usual quiet self, showing no interest in what they were doing because they introduced themselves to him as my friends. They searched until they found the clothing that I was wearing the night when I tried to open the ATM. That is when I realized that they were here on other business. I must commend them though for being so diplomatic about their work I wish more police officers would do the same. But they had a flaw, they did not use a search warrant and it was the weakness in the case. After they found the clothing, they ask me to come with them to the police station. I would like to leave this part out of it because of one too many times I made my mother sad but it is just as important to me to know that what I was doing was wrong. So they took me to my mother's house to inform her that I was going to spend the night in jail, which turned out to be nights. In fact, I spent approximately eight weeks in jail. These officers were in no hurry; they stopped and did all their chores before taking me to the station where they charged me. They charged me with Malicious Destruction of Property and Attempt to Rob and locked me up. It was a very frightening experience for me and I became a nervous wreck. I thank the other inmates who sat up with me playing cards because sleep never seemed to be an option I had. The morning came slowly and it is now time for the usual 5am shower but for me I still traumatized by the experience, but not for long. An inmate from another cell came over me while I was still sitting on the floor. He gave me the wakeup call of my life, a call that would soon turn me into a monster. He reached down with the palm of his hands and slapped me in my chest so hard you could hear it echo throughout the station and the pain was intense, I felt it for days. I quickly got up to fight back, but the thought left my mind after I was warned by my fellow inmates not to do so because things would only get worse for me. I promised myself never to let that happen again, so I prepared for the next event. Being young and full of energy and with a strong determination, the older inmates gave me their weapon. I became their "press button" someone who would do their bidding. From then on, I began beating the young and the old, the good and the bad, if they did not obey my command. After a few weeks in jail it was time for court and I understand that my Aunt Jen got me one of the best criminal defense lawyers and with that, I was offered bail the very first time I went to court. Everything is pretty much a blur from there on but what I do remember after the many court proceedings the lawyer asked me to plead guilty to the charges even as the court dropped one of the charges. The court dropped the Malicious Destruction of Property and left me with the Attempt to Rob and I got a three-year probation period. I cannot help but admit that I was clearly headed in the wrong direction driven by my desires and would do anything to satisfy my immediate needs.

I had a family to feed, I was helping my mother with the expenses for my three younger sisters and both our pockets were empty. My sister Tracy's oldest daughter Nicole also lived in to my mother's house during her school year. The enormous responsibility made me take short cuts to find immediate solutions to my problems, and attempting to break in to an ATM is just one example of how my actions made things worse for me. There were moments when I stop to think, and the thoughts of these stories imply that I was selfish and lazy but I can firmly say, that is not the case. In fact, I was never lazy and was always considering the needs of others and I am a hard working person. I was always willing to go the extra mile for my employers and I did so with sincerity.

CHAPTER FOUR

Hard Working

"It wasn't long before I learn how to work and earn
She taught me how to wash and cook
For that, I needed no book,
Her hands were the right measurement
I am the proof of her experiment
I was never too stush, for the firewood
I would have to go to the bush
For the water, I would have to go to the river,
Do that or no dinner
A time to work and a time to play
That is what my mother says
Thank God for that day".
Quote from the poem entitled, My Mother

I attended the three required schools, Pimento Walk Basic School, Ocho Rios Primary School and Ocho Rios Secondary School. During my final year at Ocho Rios Secondary School, the name changed to Ocho Rios High School and we were the first graduating class. After high school I went full time in to building construction, I spent little over a year working for my Uncle Collin. I later moved on to auto mechanics. I worked at a garage fixing cars and tire repair, I spent approximately one year in this field. After auto mechanics, I started working for a department store as assistance in the furniture department. I worked in this area for approximately two years before leaving the job. I found myself among the working class for over four years before I decided to go back to school. I later attend Adams Catering and Commercial School, where I trained as a waiter. This level of training helped me to find a job in the hotel industry where I covered approximately five years. I resigned from the hotel industry and further my studies but this time it was in theology. I attended the Caribbean Christ for the Nations Bible Institute (CCFNI). I spent almost two years studying at that institute but never graduate because I could no longer afford to school myself. After leaving the bible institute, I went out seeking for jobs, I responded to potential vacant position at a life insurance company. Part of the requirement was a written exam that requires the requisite knowledge. I studied Ordinary Long-Term and Ethics to meet the necessary requirement to become an Insurance Salesman. This never materialized because after the exams I refused the job. I will continue to share more about my working experiences as you turn these pages.

My first love for an occupation was in Auto Mechanics, but the fact that my mother could not adequately afford to send me to school, I volunteer to work with my Uncle Collin who was a building contractor, to ease the financial constraints. I went into Building Construction at the age of eleven; it was my very first job. Every summer throughout secondary school, my mother would send me off to work with my Uncle Collin on one of his construction sites. My Uncle Collin would take me with him to his various construction sites so that I could participate in the different types of manual labor that were available. I learned a lot over the years, so I became very resourceful and handy. I have knowledge in carpentry, mason, plumbing, electrical installations, tiling, manual labor, and most importantly, I am able to read and understand blueprints. The work was hard and the pay was little but I did what I had to do to send myself back to school. However, it also makes me proud to say that out of the little that I had, I was able to fulfill some of my three youngest sister's basic needs as well. I want to express an extended gratitude to my uncle who would always give me something extra whenever I fell short on school supplies, even if I had to do a few extra chores before I left his house. My mother could not afford it all on her own and the help and support needed. The truth is I enjoyed a good working relationship with my Uncle Collin. What helped me were my willingness to work accurately and my obedience.

Whether it was the work or the good relationship with my uncle, I always looked forward to my school breaks to work with him. My presence was always recognized among his staff so that they would call me by his name, and soon I became his eyes when he was absent from any given work site.

My love for auto mechanics was in no way abandoned, it got a boost while I was entering the fourth grade in high school where I received an opportunity to choose a vocational area and without a doubt auto mechanics was my pick. I later got an entry to the German Auto School after my graduation from Ocho Rios High School because of my high marks in the final exams. I could not take the offer because of my mother's financial constraints and the school was over 50 miles from home. That never stopped me from pursuing my love for auto mechanics, so as soon as I graduated from high school, I sought for a job in auto mechanics and I found one at a nearby garage, where I would assist in fixing cars and repairing tires. I can recall working on a particular car engine; in fact, it was a sedan Cortina car. I had to remove the engine in order to do the work that was required. After the work was done, the engine was held by a pulley (come-along) strapped with chains and I stood close to the engine to direct the path. As the engine slowly came into position, the chains gave way. I tried to hold the engine but the weight was too much for me, it pulled my head over and strained my back. That shattered my dreams of becoming a professional auto mechanic. I left the garage and went to work at a department store where I was the assistant to the store clerk in the furniture department. The salary was not worth talking about, so I started hustling on the side by selling a few undocumented items. This was possible because I was in charge of receiving the goods upon entry and the management's bookwork was never in good order. I soon came to realize that I was not the only one taking advantage of the untidy books. The clerk, who was a female, was doing her own buying and selling inside the store as well. I was unaware even as much as she was unaware of my doings until we went head to head in trying to sell the same item. I was returning from my lunch break, as I walked up the stairs I saw a woman standing next to the store clerk and they were talking with each other. I suddenly realized I had sold an item to that same customer. She should have picked it up the day before but did not return for it. My heart started to beat very fast as I became nervous over the fact that I was looking around the store and I could not see the item that the woman had previously bought from me. I bravely walked to them and said, "Good afternoon!" The clerk turns to me and said, "Ralston Did you sell this woman an item yesterday?" I replied, "Yes I did!" But the clerk was way ahead of me and she called the woman aside and asked her to choose another item that carries the same value of the one she bought from me yesterday and the woman did just that and that settled it but it was not over. The clerk then called me aside and began making ground rules as to how we should do business from there on; she was quick to point out to me, "Ralston, whenever you are going to make a sale like that, you should always inform me of such." What did she just said? I asked myself! I was so amazed and astonished; I just could not believe what I was hearing, especially from someone whom I had thought of as a saint. But she was always ahead of me and tactful about it. At first, I thought I was in lots of trouble because I had sold the item and put the money in my pocket. However, I realized that the clerk was doing the same thing that I was doing! It was just that she was selling an item that I had already sold the day before. It was just that her customer was picking it up earlier than mine was which should have been the other way. Because of that, we both caught on to each other and we were fortunate that the boss was unaware of our illegal activity. The lesson to be learned from this was, never doubt the ability of others to do the same thing that you are doing, and that the simplest can very well be the wisest, do not judge anyone by their appearance. The clerk was quiet and simple but she was as clever and devious. Never judge a book by its cover. Always note that the ability to steal is not limited to gender or race, it is how and when we use that ability and it may very well depend on our needs or circumstances. I started stealing because I thought it was a way out of poverty, a means to an end but it became a bad habit. Therefore, it is very important to take note of your habits because it will one day embarrass you in unexpected ways.

I gave notice, left the job at the department store, and went back to school. I had great aspiration and the department store could no longer accommodate my dreams. Furthermore, the salary was too small and I had never found contentment in stealing. I got my inspiration from my brother to go into the catering service, I saw him working in the hotel and I thought of it as a good job so I pursued it. I went to Adams Catering School where I did a two-month course in waiter training. Immediately after the course ended I was offer a job at the Almond Tree Restaurant and bar. I was employed as a bar porter because it was the only vacant position. It was a job, which I had grown to love, and later became a bartender. Working at the Almond Tree Restaurant and bar was fun while it lasted but it did not last too long. After about six months, I walked off the job because I felt pushed around a little too much or maybe I was just hot headed and impatient. Whatever it was, I will let you be the judge.

I worked the evening shift (3pm to 11pm) and was assigned to work at the swing bar where I started the shift as a Bar porter/Bartender until 5pm. This was because at any given day between 3pm to 5pm only one person would schedule to work, because it was never a busy period. As it was the break between lunch and dinner. The usual expectation failed that evening. The crowd at the bar grew in numbers but I kept smiling despite the sweat running down my face and my perspiration-soaked shirt. I was literally becoming a "hot head". My brain started working overtime to keep up with the multiple orders, ensure all the drinks got on the correct check and maintaining a balance cash register. Overall, it was a very hectic evening and I was at the very center of it. Now it was 5pm and the other Bartenders start rolling in to take up their post, as for me I was trying to close all checks. I wanted ensure that I would not end up paying for any of the checks that I had printed. The crowd was enjoying their cocktail and did not seem to be in any hurry to leave. I was supposed to leave the bar and rotate to the dining room serving as a cocktail waiter at 5:30pm so I attempted to turn over the open checks to the other bartenders whose shift had started at 5pm. They were insistent that I settle and close out all my checks before I left. It was about 5:30pm when the dining room supervisor stood on a balcony overlooking the bar and asked, "Which one of you working on the floor?" (Who is working inside the dining room?). I replied, "I am working on the floor!" My duty from 5:30pm to 11pm would have been bar porter/cocktail waiter. He glared down at me and asked, "Bishop, should you be working on the dining room floor?" and I replied, "Yes sir." He walked away and I attempted to complete closing out my checks at the bar. A few minutes later the supervisor came back and asked, "Bishop, why are you not on the floor?" I briefly explain to him what it is that I was doing and he listened and then walk away. I was stressed between the intoxicated guests, who were there to enjoy themselves and where in no hurry to leave, the lazy bartenders who would not cover for me on the dining room floor, or take over my guest checks, and an anxious and nagging supervisor breathing down my neck. Another few minutes the supervisor came back, this was his third time. He angrily asked, "Bishop why are you still not on the floor?" I just about had it. Now my head was on fire. The supervisor was on the top of the list. He never took the time out to ask what was taking me so long and I felt he could have improvised and found someone to cover for me or insisted the lazy bartenders do their job at the bar. I started spewing words at him that you cannot find in the English dictionary and I walked off the job that same moment. I only returned to collect my paycheck.

Maturity and tolerance do not come overnight it is some of the things we learn as we grow and aim to acquire overtime.

I held many jobs in the catering service since I walked off that job at the Almond Tree Restaurant and bar. I have worked at the Double VV Jerk Center, Executive banquets, private parties, Jamaica Grande Resort and other small restaurants. My job at the jerk center was an exciting job, filled with fun and excitement each day. There were live bands; live performances by the ever-slick Magician; and the food was always exceptionally great. Despite all of that, the women were the main attraction as over 90% of the staff was women and I was never going to leave out myself. During my tenure at the jerk center, I working as a bartender, I met my first adulthood girlfriend. She was much older than I was so she had experiences I was never able to match; she was short in statue but never in passion. I can never forget she had a gold tooth in her mouth, which should speak for itself, but her sexy body and pretty face had long clouded my judgment. The relationship lasted about the same time as the job and that was a little over six months. I had a dispute with my employer because I rejected the manner in which he spoke to me. So my strong resentment for bad manners drove me to walk off the job and likewise walk out of her life. The other restaurants and functions were shorter lived and not much to talk about or even remember. But the most fulfilling and the longest job I had ever held on to, was working at the Renaissance Jamaica Grande (Jamaica Grande).

I had worked at the Jamaica Grande for a little over five years before I resigned. During my tenure, I worked as a Bartender. I eventually joined the union appointed as a union delegate some few weeks later. Working at the Grande was a dream for me; it seemed that I was following in my brother's footsteps again because he had also worked at the Jamaica Grande as a Bartender. I searched for words to describe my life while working at the Jamaica Grande. The experience had many fulfilling moments and it felt like more than a dream coming true. I found love, romance, intrigue, suspense, drama, and action but most importantly and above all things, I had found a way to stop my mother from working. Providing for my mother was always my top priority and the Grande gave me that perfect opportunity. Although I cannot brag about the salary, there were always satisfied guests whom would leave a tip and it all added up. This allowed offering a greater level of assistance to my mother and my younger sisters and occasionally my older sister. I was always readily available to pay my mother's bills and meet all her financial obligations, and I did it with pride. The Jamaica Grande represents some of the greatest years it was like my time of harvest, it was very fruitful and engaged with the Union was a great opportunity. The truth is the Union had opened my eyes to see actually, what it takes to run a business. I became the king that was never crowned entertaining, always smiling and listening with the perfect response. What more could anyone ask of a bartender. All I had to do was keep the drinks coming, and this I did perfectly well or to the best of my ability. There is a lot more about the Grande, which I will reveal in chapters yet to come in this book. However, this chapter designed to place emphasis on my labor contributions and accumulated experiences. Nevertheless, after I resigned from working at the Grande, I went straight into Bible College where I would spend the next 18 months before revisiting the workforce. I will elaborate more on my time spent in Bible College in chapters to come because it was also during this same time that I got married. I applied for a job opening as a life insurance sales representative at one of the leading companies. Even though I never got past the training, my pursuit into insurance played an intricate part to my academic contribution. I must admit that all was going well, but I just could not see myself selling life insurance, so I quit while still being processed. I return to what I was good at and I found myself working at the San Souci Lido Hotel as a bartender. However, either I had stayed away too long from the catering service, or the job description was different from my previous experiences. Whatever it was, I was discourage by their work ethics and my tenure only lasted for a few days, I quit the job. I had later found myself actively engaged with many different jobs. My skills and training in building construction came in useful, allowing me to occupy many different positions in building construction. In fact, you name it and I can do it or I have done it. I would always ensure that the job done to perfection, although accomplishing the job seemed to be my main reward, because of the very little pay I often received, if any, if I paid at all.

I have always found it hard to separate my job from my women except for the writing of this book. As the saying goes, "behind every strong man, there is a good woman." There were days when I could not hold a job and my financial support would come from the woman in my life. But that does not negate the fact that I am a hard working person. I recalled hired by my father to oversee a building site that he contracted to build. He brought me into the site during the laying of the foundation, as I entered the location I immediately observed that there were too many workers employed, as there just was not enough work for that amount of staff! Being the overseer, I pointed it out to my boss (my father), and asked what he would like to be done about it? His reply was subtle and his words were few, "I will deal with it." The payday for workers was on a Friday afternoon and when he drove up, he rolled down his window, and demanded "Rally! Come here!" Without any hesitation, I walked towards his car as he handed me some brown envelopes with cash. He turned to me and said, "Pay the workers and tell some of them not to come back to work next week." He then drove away leaving me to carry out the task, but I guess that was his way of dealing with it, or it was his way of teaching me how to manage a construction site. As I handed out the envelopes, I informed the workers who should return the next week. Immediately there was an angry-murmur coming from the workers. As they express their disappointments, they began asking for the whereabouts of the Boss, and the question asked was, why he did not deliver his own decision. I had a job to do and I was doing it. From there on, I had earned the respect of the remaining workers and my father, and enjoyed a good working relationship with him.

My father to son working relationship actually began much earlier. It was after I graduated from high school and my pursuit of auto mechanics had failed me that I went in search for less strenuous jobs. My father offered me a position as a conductor collecting fares on one of his buses. I took the job and began working on the bus that travel from Ocho Rios to Brown's Town or there were times when we would travel from Ocho Rios to Kingston. Neither route was ever my concern, because I enjoyed the adventure or even the 5am that I would get out of bed in order to be on time for work. What became my main concern was the fact that I had to stay with my father in order to catch the bus at 5am in the morning. I never felt welcome and there was too much distance between us. My other concern was the fact that there seems to be no growth in being a conductor and my father did not seem to have a single concern about my welfare, just his money. Therefore this was short-lived as it lasted approximately two months, I took my clothes in small portions until enough was left for one go and I left his house and job quietly. As rude as it may sound, I did not notify my father or justify my reason for leaving his house and quitting his job. Maybe my father had good intentions but he never took the time out to ask me what it is that I truly wanted and I never could find the courage to share my dreams and desires. I want to emphasize the importance of communication in every relationship; communication is the most important element in every relationship and our father/son relationship was lacking that important element. **We should never assume that what we are doing is that which needed simply because it seems good.** We should never try to interpret someone else emotions or needs instead we should seek clarification through communication.

After I had explored different career and meaningless jobs, I finally found something that I had a passion for and this was farming. I later became my own boss. I set up a small farm where I would raise six-week-old chickens and pigs. It was during this same period, I opened a grocery shop and bar. All of this was during my final few years before I went to prison. The grocery shop and bar did not last very long, it closed down while I was in jail but my farm survived until this day, although I am just raising pigs. The farm would not have survived either had it not been for help of my sister Tamara, who kept it going while I was in prison. I cannot thank her enough for keeping my dreams alive. I refused to eat their meat or any part that comes from a pig and it is no surprise why. I have now grown to love my farm animals with a passion. Being around the animals has given me an opportunity to understand them while learning their behavior patterns. I also learned how to help them give birth when they have difficulty and administrating the right medication according to their illnesses. On the other hand, as crazy as it may sound, I have learned how to communicate with them in a way that they understand and follow my simple instructions. It may seems like I am bragging about my farm but I have earned the right because it is one of the few places or the few things I do that I feel happy doing.

I could continue to brag about my farm or working experiences but I am not the type of person who believes in all work and no play, in fact my mother had long ago told me that there is a time and place for everything. It is clear that I am not all about the fun or pleasures of life but it is also clear that when it is time to party I am more than ready I am prepared. Now let us play.

CHAPTER FIVE

Time to play

"A time to work and a time to play,
that's what my mother says
Thank God for that day"
Quote from the poem entitled, My Mother

Ever since I can remember, I have always enjoyed my own company or being by myself and this has followed me from childhood into adulthood even unto manhood. As a child, I would play out in the streets with my homemade toys by myself. When I was not doing that, I would be off hunting for fruits in the woods, again all by myself. The truth is growing up as a child, the company of others I would scarcely enjoy. Since we are on the subject of fruits, I should let you know that I would not rest at night if I knew that a fruit tree was ready for harvesting and I did not get any during the day. Climbing a fruit tree at night might seem as a dangerous act but for me then, that was more than enough fun.

It is said, "Happiness is a state of mind" but for me that is far from the truth. I would agree with anyone who believes that "contentment is a state of mind" but I firmly believe that happiness is an outward experience working inwardly often times on the mind. Even so, it did not derive from thoughts of the mind. If I may be so bold, happiness is the fulfillment of a physical or emotional desire. While on the other hand the source of contentment comes from the mind and can only be satisfied in the mind. I truly believe that we should never worry about the things that we lack in life, but it is with that same breathe that I say, without those things, there is not much to be happy about neither. When you are poor, the presumption of happiness is a thought rather than a thing. If you are not able, emancipate yourself from that mental scar you remain in poverty. I have learnt to make myself satisfied with little but I will never be happy knowing that I do not have enough. I have grown past the days when playing with my homemade toys and hunting for fruits was my only source of fun, and progress to a more mature type of fun. There were movies, clubs, dancehalls, gambling casinos, beaches and the list goes on. In between the fun, there was always me being me, just staying home listening to some music or enjoying myself in my kitchen cooking a meal. I must admit that I was never much of a sports fan. Therefore, I did not find myself attached to any of those activities except for every fourth year when the World Cup football or the Olympics were happening. During that time, my TV would be the only thing that I am glue to, because I could never afford to attend any of these live games. Sports were not the only thing I watched on television, I always enjoyed watching cartoons and animated films or a good action movie would always get my attention. In the early days, Western (cowboy) and Karate movies were the most popular movies. Unfortunately, options for viewing were never an option for me because it was always pay-for-view. I would always pay for viewing someone else's screen whether it is cash or kind favors. This was because I grew up in a home where there was no TV. At home, all we had was an AM and FM band radio that seldom played because of the lack of electricity in the earlier days. The view from outside of the neighbor's window was always good enough for me but not because I would not go inside to watch. The opportunity not always an option, but even the view from outside came at some expense to me. There was always chore that they need me to do and coincidentally, it was always before my favorite cartoons. I believe that was the catch. When my mother needed to watch her favorite show, we would walk almost a mile in the dark just to get to her friend's house but it was a small price to pay for watching the TV even if it was in black and white. Then there was the community theater, which frequently showed movies on weekends. Although I was not always financially able to pay my entrance fee, I would still find other means of watching the movie. I can clearly remember one particular night after not having any money to pay my way. I chose the next best option, which was to climb an ackee tree that would give me a clear view inside of the theater and it was within listening range. As I began to climb the ackee tree, I slipped and my right leg caught in the barbwire that was a part of the fencing. The barbwire stapled on to the ackee tree and it cut through my pants and into my flesh at the back of my leg. There was blood all over my foot but that did not stop me from watching the movie that night. I continued to climb the ackee tree to find my favorite seat, sat down and enjoyed the movie. I guess it goes to show that nothing is in fact free, because although I had no money to pay the entrance fee for the movie it cost me some blood and pain with a scar to tell the tales. As the years went by my life became more abundant and I could finally pay for the things that I enjoyed in life, which included actually paying cash to watch a movie.

Gambling was a big thing for me in my teenage years even during school sessions. In fact, the slightest school break became an opportunity to gamble. The games would range from dominoes, card games or just anything where a bet wagered could be, even my class work. The one who scored the highest mark won. Then there were the poker boxes, which taught me a valuable lesson after I lost all the money that I had been saving to buy a pair of shoes. It taught me to spend my money wisely and to spend it on what it budgeted for. I also learned that gambling is a form of greed that could lead to stealing. Among all the lessons most importantly, I had learned never to play another poker box again.

The alcohol and ganja walked hand in hand with all that was taking place. Although it was customary for a bartender to drink alcohol, for me the ganja would add its own weight to any given occasion. There were nights when I would go from one club to the next searching for a good time or I just wanted to party. However, what I found to be strange is that, in this era in my life I seldom remember all the actual events, all I seem to remember is that I felt like a king waiting to be crowned. My room was the scent of money; my car was among the most expensive that money could buy in line with my status and age. My clothes were the finest and I wore name bran cologne, handpicked by the woman in my life. I had relationships that often times came with a question mark. However, my family was never bold enough to ask, so there were many unanswered questions as it relates to a few of my relationships. Nevertheless, I was living the life so I never consider the consequences. Coupled with all of that, I was a great dancer, one that would easily draw the attention of a crowd, usually that would be after I had finished my spliff (ganja rolled in paper) and the alcohol kicked in, yes, you guess right, I was high. This is not to discredit my natural ability to dance because with or without the ganja and alcohol I could make my moves and Michael Jackson's dance moves were my favorite. It was just that the ganja and alcohol made it seem much easier. Despite my craving for fun in that era of my life, there was one thing that I never found to be entertaining and that was strip clubs. I can only recall going into one in my lifetime and it was a very short stay. It was on a night after me and some of my friends had left a party, and the night was still young. They had decided that they were going to a strip club and I went along for the fun. As we got to the entrance one of the crewmembers walked up to the security. Whatever he had said was enough for all of us to gain entrance and it certainly seems like he was no stranger. When we got inside some of the crew walked over to the stage where the girls were dancing, but I took a seat by the bar and ordered a drink. After I received my drink, I later asked for my bill, the bartender who is a female told me the cost for the drink. I placed the money on the counter and began sipping on my drink, and when I glanced to see what was going on at the stage I saw that there were girls dancing and removing elements of their clothes. I realized that it did not take much to fill my eyes, and within a few minutes, I began to feel uncomfortable so I decided to leave. I got up and walked out. The next day my friends saw me and asked why I left so soon. The answer I gave was simple but the truth, it just was not my thing, that was the first, and last time I had ever visited a strip club.

I was never a big dancehall fan either; somehow, I just did not feel comfortable. I am not sure if it was the atmosphere or the people that are associated with dancehalls. Whatever it is, I was on edge once I entered a dancehall and that limited my ability to have fun. I pretty much stayed away from any such events, with a few exceptions. I do recall going to a live stage show called the *Bob Marley Birthday Bash*. I wanted to listen and see the Marley's performance and they did put on a good show. There was a break before the featured event and I decided to make myself a bed and take a nap. The shouting coming soon awakened me from the crowd as the MC made his introductions for the featured event, who was Sanchez.

The crowd went wild; there were screams everywhere even as Sanchez began singing his first song, for me it was money well spent because the performance was great. Nevertheless, despite disliking the dancehall atmosphere, I hosted a few shows myself. Maybe I missed a key sign here because I seemed to have a stroke of bad luck with my shows. They would turn out either fair or at a loss. As I recall, the first show that I hosted was in my own community, and it was in the time when money was no obstacle for me. I hired two sound systems to play on that night. All the drinks, liquor and food were in place, the weather was perfect and the dance got off to an early start but something bad happened and spoiled it all. The party came to a halt after the electricity went out. Numerous attempts made to have the electricity restored, but the hours slowly drifted away until I learned that it would not be possible to restore the electricity. That was the end of a good party and thousands of dollars, but I was still determined to put on a good party. I decided to try it again and I went and hired another big sound system but I had my party in another community at a more popular venue. I printed my flyers properly and made my bookings to promote the event. The food, liquor and other beverages were readily available. Regrettably, it was another disappointing day and night for me because the rain began falling at 10am in the morning and fell right throughout day until 7pm the evening. Because of the great publicity and the positive feedback that I got for the party, I decided we were going to make it happen according to the plan. The rain fell in intervals so I used the opportunity to prepare the food with assistance of a few hired hands. So we were ready for the party but not without more disappointment. The sound system did not show up until after 8pm, and by the time they were ready to play it was almost 10pm. With the rain continuing to fall and the late sound system, I was off to a failing start and that is exactly the way it ended. There went a few more thousands of dollars and another failed party. Those were not the last but as I said, I had a streak of bad luck and the other parties were either fair or at a loss. I tried! I did try.

For everything, there is a season and my life is very seasonal or should I say has many memorable moments. My era of club life and parties is no exception, to the days of gambling, although short lived, it was one for the records and it is these combined moments why I am who I am today. I must admit to myself that I am a very slow learner or I do not read the warning signs of life careful enough. Even when the writing was on the wall, I ignored it, as if it was not there. I will continue to emphasize that everything has a price and we will only get what it is we are willing and able to pay for, nothing more nothing less. However, to say that there are no exceptions to the rule is not what I mean. You may call it luck and I would agree, but for me, the only luck I have ever known is bad luck. So for me the rule applies itself to every area of my life, I reap what I have sown.

The saddest days of my life

This is my view, in the midst of life, there is laughter and sadness and at the end of it all, there is death. I have had my fair share of laughter and equal to none, my fair share of sadness. Being plague with a burdensome life both of my hands broken, on separate occasions, my left leg broken and wounded during the same period as my right arm. I had car accident after car accident, falling from an upstairs building while I was painting a window on a ladder, corrective surgery on my left arm and leg although separate incidents but the list goes on. It is never the easiest task to remember some of my tragic moments in fact my heart cries even as I type these words, so where do I start? Let me start with my very first car accident, it was on a night when I was hosting a party on the beach and I had to leave suddenly. One of my closest friends gets into a quarrel with one of my associates and seeing that my friend was high on ganja and drunk, I decided to take him home. I held onto his hand, placed him inside the car and drove off. As we reached the main road, he became boisterous, so I tried to calm him down by talking to him but he opened the door and put his left leg outside. I immediately grabbed onto him but he resisted with the force of a hurricane. Consequently, I lost control of the car as it swerved across the road into a church wall. I swiftly got out of the car to check on my friend who was lying unconscious on the ground. Realizing that he was not responding, I stopped a passing taxi and rushed him to the hospital. While we were at the hospital, the doctors told me that I was the one who needed medical care and my friend just needed rest so that he could sleep off the level of alcohol and drugs that were in his system. I was not so lucky, my right arm fractured and needed a plaster cast and the car, which I had borrowed, was in need of repair. I had many more car accidents prior to this one. But none of them was as serious as this one. On the other hand, should I say none that gave me any serious injury? Although the cars were damage to a greater extent. An old Jamaican proverb says, "Bredda Annancy seh, two troubles is better than one." What brother Annancy had said may have worked out for him but certainly not for me! It was about two months later I received a severe injury that was not associated to a car accident. I remember the night that I was ambush and my left leg chopped as if it was happening right now. It all started on the morning when I asked one of my cousins to take my current girlfriend home to pick up some of her stuff. Later that evening I accompanied them back to the house. We stood outside the car as we waited for her to return. A man confronted us and asked if we were there earlier in the morning. He was inquiring because his car had been park on the street earlier when another car had put a dent in it and drove off without notification. The driver, my cousin, told him although he had been there earlier he did not dent his car. The man then turned and called for the witnesses who allegedly saw what took place. They all gave their record of the event, including a little boy who appeared to be only five years old. My cousin became boisterous as he defended himself and began shouting even at the little boy whom he repeatedly called a liar. Seeing that the conversation was going nowhere I intervened and begin to work out an amicable solution. I decided that I would accept the cost of the damage if it would bring peace between the two parties. The man heeded to my arguments as I suggested we look at the damage and do an estimate on the cost for repair. We all agreed to look at the damage but his car was at another location. For that reason, I asked him to get inside my cousin's car and accompany us to view his car where it was park, he agreed. Before he got into the car, he called out for someone to be his personal company so we waited a while for that person to come forward. The man received comfort by the fact that my girlfriend also decided to come along for the ride because he knew her better than my cousin and me so the issue of trust was resolved. We had to travel at a slow speed because the surface of the street was very rocky when suddenly I heard a loud bang on the car as if someone had hit it with something solid and heavy. Within seconds, I saw someone stabbing at my cousin with a machete. The person was at the driver's window, making numerous attempts to either cut or stab him. My cousin jumped across the front seat, landed on me, opened the door, and made a swift escape before I even knew what was happening!

The car was a standard (manual transmission), so the moment he removed his foot off the clutch and brake, it automatically stopped. The person with the machete ran after my cousin in the street towards the main road. Meanwhile, my girlfriend and the other man got out of the car. By the time I got out of the car, thrown stones were coming from various directions. There were shouts coming from my girlfriend and the owner of the other car, begging the men who were throwing stones to stop, but no one would listen. Within a few moments, the owner of the other car fell before me as one of the stones hit him on his head. My main concern was looking out for my girlfriend and my own safety. So I pulled her aside and put up a challenge with the men who were throwing stone while returning a few in the direction from which they came. Vigorously defending we I had forgotten that one of the men had gone after my cousin with a machete and my back was now turn in his direction. That is when I felt a chop to my left leg. At first it felt like I got hit with a hard instrument, then I felt the warm blood running down my leg telling me that it was more than hit. There was an unusual sensation coming from my leg but my mind would not allow me to attend to it because of the battle that was before me. The person wielding the machete was like a little mongrel dog that would bite retreat because he ran as if he was the one that was in danger. Now I had a wounded leg, a wounded man lying on the ground, a girlfriend to protect, three men throwing stones at me and one man running around like a mongrel dog with a machete. The neighbors who knew my girlfriend and the man that was lying unconscious came to their rescue and I made a run for it. As I ran through the rocky street, I fell into a gutter alongside the road and landed on my once broken hand. Nevertheless, I made my way to the main road where an owner of a pickup van came to my rescue. He drove me to the nearest police station and from there to the hospital. There are questions that surrounded that incident and speculations that I try to avoid. The questions that are at the forefront of my mind are; why did my cousin jump out of the car when he could have driven away? After all the car belonged to me, so why would he run and leave me behind? Whom were they really trying to hurt? The very same person who called for help was lying in front of me unconscious and it seemed like they had no intention at all to hurt my girlfriend. I know I am not that forgiving but the matter is settled and what is done is done. Although I have had corrective surgery and therapy on my leg, that chop left me with a scar and a limp for life so it is a constant reminder of the event.

Another injury came after falling from a ladder while painting my uncle's window. This particular incident is very bewildering and you are soon to understand why. I had been living at my uncle's house for over five years. This was about a year after my grand uncle had died and my Uncle Carlos, my mother brother had asked me to be the caretaker for his property while he was still living in England. I got up early in the morning as I always did; only this morning my mind was set on painting the windows. So I brought out the ladder because the windows were on the top floor of the house above the garage. Before I was ready to paint, I put some security measures in place. I got some rope and tied it to the ladder unto the balusters of the upstairs veranda, just to limit the movement of the ladder while I painted. So my security measures were in place and double-checked. My paint and paint brushes were at hand, I climbed the ladder and started painting the windows and just as I was about to finish the third window pane I felt the ladder move underneath my feet and before you know it, I fell to the ground. I went down with a skillful landing but my left hand took the weight of my body hence the bones in my wrist were dislocated. My uncle came home shortly after. When he arrived, I was sitting in the garage holding my hand that is in pain with paint splashed all over the walls and my body. He asked me to explain to him what happened so I did, but he could not come to terms with what I was saying because the ladder was still tied and intact, and I did not have an explanation. My wrist was damage so bad that it needed corrective surgery; there goes another painful experience as if my left leg was not enough. I must say thanks to the hard working doctors who did a perfect job on my arm and leg to them, I am grateful and to all the medical practitioners who continued to save and enhance lives, I give thanks for a job well done. I could go on and on writing about my tragic moments or sad days but I am saving a few for short stories to share when I am much older.

There was a time in my life when things would only "get from bad to worse." When I thought that, my injuries were more than enough there were more traumatizing experiences. The sudden death of my younger sister Tameka gave me a shock to my brain. Her death happened during the time when I was nursing the chop wound to my left leg, so I was unable to go about my own business freely and Tameka was on the top of my list for support. Tameka was a very bright and beautiful young woman. She loved to read and her smile would light up the room. It was after a massive rainfall had caused a landslide one afternoon, I received a call that my sister trapped in a car, and she was only 18 years old. I was even more devastated when I learned they had also removed the body of my Aunt Jen, my father's sister who was also my nurse and scheduled to visit me the next morning. I was lost in the moment after hearing the sad news about my sister who I loved dearly. By the time I arrived, they had taken her lifeless body from the car; memories of that moment still make me want to cry. Somehow, I found my way to the hospital after swearing at everyone who was standing in my way or would not move fast enough. Reaching the hospital, I requested to see my sister, but as the porter remove the cloth from her lifeless body I broke down in tears. I do not recall anything that happened after that, only what others told me. They remember seeing and hearing me hitting and swearing at everybody that stood close to me or even tried to console me. They told me that the doctors at the hospital had to restrain me by giving me medication for me to rest, everything from there on is history never forgotten. Another great lost that I had suffered was the death of my eldest sister Tracy, occurred during my time in prison, so I was unable to attend her funeral. I was saddened by her death and even more so that I was unable to pay my last respects. My mother's death also left me with many regrets, even to this very day and I truly wish she were around to see and to read this book. However, the last time I saw her face I remember it like it was yesterday, she was lying on her hospital bed. As I fed her some Ensure that my sister Tamara had bought for her; she sipped a little and refused the rest of it. Not knowing that this would be her last meal, I heeded to her request even as she mumbled the last words I would ever hear from her, "leave me alone." Since it was late in the evening, I headed home and the next morning I got a call from the hospital that I urgently needed. But there were no urgency required because she had already died, they just needed me to sign off on her death and call a funeral home to receive her body. I met my sisters Tamara at the hospital after I went to escort my younger sister Tosanna who was unaware of our mother's death. I wanted everyone to take one last look of her face before they took her body away and I was equally anticipating the same. When

I saw the look on her face, it was as if she was smiling and at peace. In a lifetime, one can go through so many and no more but I believe I had lived through two-life times, although I have not yet completed one.

In the span of 5 years, I went from fun and laughter to sadness and tears. I went from rags to riches, the underground king to serving King Jesus and from weakness to strength. All these moments in my life led me to Christianity, a search for a new hope and new life nevertheless, here begins a new era in my life. However, how could I end the fun or sadness without talking about some of the women in my life? Some of which have played a very influential part in the happiness in my life but some of which had destroyed everything that I ever dreamed for with very little hope in sight.

CHAPTER SIX

Lovers and Friends

Earlier I had said, "Truth is in every written word" in this book, I will keep my promise. Before I go into the details of this chapter, I want to lay a foundation of basis on which I would like to be judge. I am a Jamaican with rich African heritage. Growing up with a single parent did not allow me the privilege to know what it is like to have father around or any male figure in the home. This is common among the Jamaican people especially among the poorer class. I could easily say it is a part of our Jamaican culture for a man to have more than one woman. Take my father for an example, he has five children, four of which I am certain, they belonged to four different mother one which he later married. I do not intentionally seek to single out my father because I am aware of the view that over 50 percent of the Jamaican children were born to a single parent. I do not seek to justify or endorse this act but the reality I cannot deny. There is an expressed view that most Jamaican men are terrified my marriage, some even see it as being weak. It is allege that "Jamaica is a Christian country" but I have my doubts about that allegation. Despite "Jamaica have more churches per square mile in the world" according to the Guinness book of records, a large percentage of our local artist write lyrics that is contrary to the Christian principles. Furthermore, a larger percentage acts in a manner, which is far from that which expected of a Christian. Again, I am not trying to justify or endorse those actions but I will not deny them. Therefore, I want to attribute this behavioral pattern to a culture that exists among the Jamaican people and since we did not adopt it in the western world, I would like to trace it back to our rich African heritage. I grew up in that culture in fact; nurtured by it and became a part of it. I share the view that, "You cannot make an omelet without breaking an egg," you cannot find a solution without creating a problem. I had chosen to embrace that culture hence I would not break the cycle until 5 years ago when I accepted that there is a better life. Now on the basis that I wish to be judged, I do not wish to be judged as a Christian. The earlier years of my life would not reflect that despite my regular attendance at church. Although I baptized some fourteen years ago, the process of transformation was a very long one. I do not wish to be judge as being wise because I had done some foolish things. I do not wish to be judge as a discipline child because my mother is not aware of most of my actions. It is said that, "children live what they learn," I started working at age 11 leave my mother's home at age 17 so I never spent much time learning from my mother because I spent more time on the street. My learning is a survival instinct "street smart." I will do what it takes to survive and to impress my pairs. However, a major part of that learning entangled in the non-Christian side of the Jamaican culture "men should have a lot of women." Therefore, if I am to be judge, judge me by my culture and accept the fact that I am a changed man.

In my opinion, the hardest distinction to make between a male and female relationship is, where friendship ends and lovers begin. I felt this is a result of the emotional bonds, which are usually involved in both aspects of the relationship.

I remember my first girlfriend very well, friends we were but never lovers. At age 9, we could not tell the difference because we were too young and still playing a game of dolly house. Yet still we attached emotionally in our friendship. Or my second girlfriend who would hide from school with me just so that we could spend the day together. Emotionally we had something going on and we were the best of friends but never lovers. In earlier days, a girlfriend was an occasional innocent kiss from a girl who is simply a friend. We knew very little about sex and even though we were born with the right tools, we had a long way to go before we would start using them. Times were different then. We had strict parental guidance, very limited access to the media as TV was not a popular thing, and radio was restricted to good music with less sexual lyrics. Now sex is highly publicized and just looking at the opposite sex tends to have sexual meaning. But could it be prophecy fulfilling as these words unfold "what was hidden from the wise and prudent, is now revealed to the babe and suckling." As I grew older, the word girlfriend took on a different meaning; it went from an emotionally friendship to an innocent kiss for incentive to love making. I do not think that I was any different from the many that had childhood fantasies and dreams. Fantasies and dreams of a beautiful and wonderful life, someone who would love me with all their heart, a home filled with laughter and the blessings of God Almighty. I would soon have to wake up to a harsh reality.

I first stumbled across love during my final years in high school when I met up with a girl who had me wrapped around her little finger! I was the usual shy boy with very little to say but there was always a captivating smile on my face that must had warmed her heart. So there she was, dark skin, carved out shape, natural hair and eyes that made my heart melt. We would play with each other as if we were both our favorite toy. Although I was a few years older than she was, the difference in our age was not significant to our relationship except for the fact that I helped her with her schoolwork. I would always choose a fine gift for her birthdays and chocolate for just about any occasion. Her lips were soft and breath as fresh as the morning breeze, each time I embraced her it felt like the very first. Our relationship was short lived after she moved away and the distance between us put a dent into our teenage love.

Still shy or "slow" as I was once told, it has always been a challenge for me to find the right words to say and even when I think of them, they just will not come out of my mouth. So it was always hard for me say, what I wanted to say to the girl who I wanted and for that I kept missing my chances and opportunities to be with a girl that caught my eye. Therefore, I would end up being the one that chosen by a woman instead of being the one who chooses. As I grew older, I became wiser and although I was still slow, I was able to choose the woman and women that I desired.

I was young, single and considered attractive by most people's standards and all I had to do was read between the lines to pick up on a woman's clues. While living at my Uncle Clem's house, my next-door neighbor had a serious crush on me. It was my first few months working at the Jamaica Grande and I could not enter or leave the house without being notice. Despite the fact that I was single, I never see a long-term relationship with her but I decided to get involved with her. She entered my life at a time when my focus was on my new job and supporting my family was my priority. She started visiting me on a regular basis until the relationship had run its course. While working at the Jamaica Grande Beach Resort I was on top of my game living a dream because my life had taken an exceptional turn and it was my time to shine. I was meeting people from many different parts of the world, my financial outlook was starting to change and I became even more attractive to women. However, among the things that I had learned was, one thing is for sure, it is hard to encounter so many different people and not find friendship although for me I found much more.

There she was sitting at my bar counter sipping on her drink as I attended to the other existing customers I would watch her out of the corner of my eye. She sat with two friends, and I tried to be professional since I was still on duty and I could lose my job if found flirting with a guest. So we laughed at each other jokes even as I tried to be entertaining to all the other customers. I assumed that she like me because she sat there and waited until my shift ended. I later learned that one of the women that she was with was her sister. Illegal as it was for a bartender to walk the beach at night with a guest, there I was holding her hand thanking God. I also thanked God that it is now legal to hold the hands of a white woman. The night was very quiet and all you could hear was the sea rushing to the shore and the cool breeze blowing creating a romantic atmosphere. We walked until we came up on a nice spot that was very private so we sat there and became further acquainted with each other. I reached out to her and she responded in like manner and we had our first kiss but that kiss was more than incentive, it ignited a wet beach and turned a cool night into a furnace. The thought of getting a room must have crossed her mind but for me I did not want to let the flame go out and an employee would have never been allowed in to a guest's room. Lucky for us there was no one else around. By the time, we were done; our burning emotions had turned in to sweat and the cool ocean breeze on the beach was now warm. The moment was new, exciting and wild so wild that we spent almost the rest of the night searching for a gold ring, which she had been wearing on her finger. The night ended without notice and the morning was swiftly upon us. Sadly, she had come to the end of her vacation. It was her final day in Jamaica, her flight was within a few hours, she was in no mood to leave, and I did not want her to go. I embraced her as I watched her lips trembling and the tears running down her face, we kissed as we tried to say goodbye to each other, exchanged addresses and telephone numbers and we went our separate ways. From that moment, I realized what it was to break an employee's code of conduct and I had tasted the bitter sweet of racism as I had now learned that we are one people no matter color or race. This was my first time being with a woman of different color and race but what made it special is that she wanted me as much as I wanted her. From that moment on, our love began to grow even with the distance between us. However as I began to reflect on the past week, for six days out of her one week vacation she sat at my bar and would have a drink and I never made a move on her. Just a smile and the best service money can buy but as I said, I am slow because she was right there in front of me and I still could not find the right words to say to her.

We would talk for hours on the phone at night and we exchanged letters through the postal mail to make the distance seem shorter. It was as if she was right next door and it was only another six months later and she was back in my arms again. Our love grew and lasted for a few years, as it would no longer stand to the test of the distance that was between us. Our own priorities were at the forefront so we went from lovers to friends. The reality was that she had no intention of living in Jamaica and I had no intention of living in the states.

Life will grant us our heart desires if we are willing to pay the price but we must always be sure of what it is that we desire. We must acknowledge it when we receive it or else it will be gone before we actually benefit from it because **it takes twice the strength to preserve than it is to achieve**. I went from a boy with a dream to a man that was living that dream. I could not see pass my ego and hard heartedness "my way or the highway" so I ended many relationships that were worth keeping. I saw wealth and prosperity inside my home and I forgot to close the door to keep it in, so it walked straight out the door even as I watched helplessly. I was helpless because I did not try to preserve what I had by acknowledging and making the necessary assessment of what I had. I was defenseless when I lost it. If you do not know what you have, you will not know what you are losing. However, hope is always on the way and mine would soon be within reach.

Not in the form of a second chance but as an opportunity realized. Or one that I slowly took up.

My journey with women was not always a bed of roses. There were many with thorns and there were instances where their thorn pierced me deep leaving me with a permanent scar I will never live to forget. From a very early age, my mother taught me to give thanks for all things. However, among all the women that I had and regrettable did so there is one that remains at the top of that list. She was my kind of girl, sexy, dark skinned, hardworking and intelligent! She had more than a crush on me and the fact that she was living 5 minutes away made it easy because I had just ended a long distance relationship. I was single with no children and she promised to change all of that, she offered the one thing I needed most, a child. I was excited to be a father and the fact that she already had children I thought it would be much easier for me. She walked straight through the front door; she did not have to knock because it was wide open. Everything was perfect she knew exactly what to do to keep me satisfied and her never hesitated not even for a moment, and I obviously made her happy because she kept coming back for more. My front door was always open until I tragically closed it. She was not who she said she was and she was not living the life she said she was living and I was involve right in the middle of it all. She could not have any more children and she was not single our relationship lasted about one month but the scar remain. She left a thorn in my flesh that I will never forget because I have unfulfilled desire (a child to call my own).

I could speak of the many disappointing moments I had with women but I find it unnecessary at this time and I believe that would need a book for itself. I do acknowledge that there are many who would see me as being a wicked person and some women are no better than Delilah is. Nevertheless, I try to stay positive and focus mainly on the good aspects of life or the most enjoyable memories.

Shortly after this tragedy I met Suzette. Suzette and I were living in separate homes and our relationship filled with uncertainty. She was still living in the home that belongs to the father of her two children. On the day, that I received the chop wound and fractured arm. The following day she was schedule to leave for work on the crew ship. While I was in the hospital nursing my chop wound she came to visit before she board her flight, tears were running down her face as she watched me lying on my back unable to walk around because of the severity of my chop wound. It was while I was in the hospital, I learned that my right arm was fracture from the fall I had taken while running away from my attackers. So to make matters worse my left leg was unable to move and my right arm was wrapped and awaiting plaster cast. She poured out her sympathy in as much word as she could, while pondering if she should leave me in the hospital to care for myself, I told her I would be ok and she was free to go. She left for the crew ship. At this time I want to say thanks to Aunt Lora my Uncle Carlos's wife who made sure my needs were met. Thanks to Aunt Jen my father's sister who nurse my chop wound. Special thanks to my sister Tameka who did my chores and died while doing so. Suzette started her job on the cruise ship and would be away for months. I continue nursing the wound on my left leg and my fractured right arm. I thought that with her not being around all the time was the missing piece in our relationship, but it was much more than just that. Among my many visitors, Ava appeared and the moment was breath taking.

This is what I remember; I was lying in bed one afternoon nursing my chop wound to my leg and my fractured arm. I could not move around freely, it was then I received a call from her saying that she would like to come and visit me. Being the courteous and nurturing type, she asked if she could bring some chicken soup for me and my answer was yes without any hesitation. She arrived in khaki short jeans and a polo blouse and slippers on her feet. Her cologne was her usual exquisite smell. She dressed simple but effective. She smiled with sadness beneath as if she was grieving for my situation. She handed me the chicken soup so I sat up to drink it. This was an unusual thing for me because normally I would not eat a home cooked meal from a woman who was a partial stranger. I had only known her as my co-worker. She was a cashier at the Jamaica Grande, but she was exceptional because she was my heart desire. I not only knew her, she was a part of heart. If only she knew how many times, I had dreamt of a moment with her. If she only knew that every time I am near her, her scent pulled me closer. I would stare at her as she walked to her workstation, holding her cash pan slightly below her armpit. Even as she walks delicately without effort, my lips were seal, as the words could not find their way out. I never got around to truly expressing my feelings. She sat beside me on the bed that day and watched me as I finished the soup. She then removed the bowl and we chatted for a while, as her presence brought me comfort. She was not very good on jokes, so there was not much laughter but I cannot emphasize enough how her presence made me feel. Now it was time for her to go and as she was about to say goodbye, I raised my head up and kissed her on the cheek. She got up and left for her home. About an hour later my phone rang, she was on the line. "What just happened?" She asked!

"What do you mean?"

"Did you just kiss me?"

"Yes! But I am sorry if I had crossed the line!"

"No! You did not but I just was not expecting that to happen."

The conversation ended in a brief moment, but not in my mind because I was even more confident about her than ever before. I knew that the next time I saw her, I would be breaking my sealed lips, even if it's only with another kiss. So she did come back and visited me after numerous calls to her phone and long conversations, which she always seemed to dominate. However, I did not mind one bit, I was more concerned about my chances of seeing her again. There was never a day that went by that I did not need her. Even the days when she refused to see me, I would come crawling as if her insults were an invitation. She had always been on my mind from the first day I laid eyes on her but she was a hard catch and even harder to keep. However, you know me, I am slow and patience is not one of my strong attributes. Therefore, it made our relationship even more difficult but as I had said, she came to me when I needed her most.

Suzette was working her job on the cruise ship and had gone for eight months at a time, there was some distance between us. At first, it seemed like a good opportunity to me, so I helped her prepare for the trip. However, looking back on it I needed to ask myself, would I choose opportunity over responsibility? I believe that at some point in our lives we could be call upon to make this choice, but note this; we reap what we sow. I don't wish to be selfish and I could not ask her to stay, we had just started dating and neither of us know for sure our level of commitment, furthermore she had her two sons to take care of and everything was happening too fast. Nevertheless, choosing an opportunity to bring you financial success but only at the expense of your responsibility does not always walk hand in hand. If you leave your responsibility unmanned, someone will do it for you and you may not reap the benefit that may derive from it. Then again it's a choice we all have to make but always consider the risk that is involved and what it is that you are willing to give up to get what you want. Even to the point of which is more important to a sustainable life. Her choice was clear; she had chosen opportunity and lost her responsibility. I cannot ignore the fact that my ability to speak up or me being slow was always a hindrance in my relationships but because of it, I am often misunderstood.

Nevertheless my wish was granted, Ava visited me again and I opened my sealed lips and sealed our friendship with a breathtaking kiss, only this time she was more than ready as her tender lips pressed against mine creating a romantic mood and an unforgettable moment. We grew from friends to lovers and she became the lady of my life. It was in her arms that I had found true comfort and when she kissed me, it felt like there was no ending to her passion, which was wild but gentle. When it came down to making love, she had an addiction for details so she would always ensure that it was perfect. She had qualities that fulfilled my every desire of a woman and there were times when the very thought of her silky skin and her warm body touching against mine, would trigger every muscle in my body. I could never be too close to her not to miss her and no matter what caused us to argue I would always be the first one try to make amends. The truth is, I loved her then and I love her even more now. However, although my passion burns for her until this day we have had our good moments and bad moments. I cherish the good moments the bad ones were noticeable. There were times when I thought that she did not want my love or I was receiving punishment for all the wrongs other men have done to her. She would make it seem so easy to shut me out of her life or even say words that would cut through me like a laser, with no regards of my feelings. Not to say, I was a saint, but I always hold the fear of a committed relationship with her because she seems to find it much easier to close her door on me than to open it. However, I would always come knocking and waiting for the moment when she would be ready for someone like me, a man of few words and a thorn in his flesh. The distance between me and Suzette create the perfect opportunity for us. But our relationship became shaky after Suzette came for her vacation and stayed with me at my Uncle Carlos's house where I was living at the time. Ava suggested that I keep my distance and I was growing weary of arguing with her. Like I said, I am no saint and it is hard to choose love over love. After the chop wound on my leg and my fractured right arm healed, I did corrective surgery on my left leg and I went back work. I baptized and later tended my resignation to go to Bible College. Christians are required to marry especially when you are potential student in Bible College. I proposed to Suzette because I thought she would suite me best as a wife as for Ava I was still not sure if she was ready to be committed to someone like me. Like every woman that came into my life, Ava had her share of problems with me; the only difference was all she had to say jump and I would simply ask how high. She was my heart desire but her pride was too high she could not climb over it and I was slow in letting her know.

Getting married was always a part of my dreams, I thought of it as an honorable thing to do and after I became a Christian, it was even more required of me to do so. Therefore, when the opportunity presented itself I held on to it.

I got married at a time when my life had taken a paradox shift, I no longer felt like I was in the driver seat. I was on either autopilot or awaiting instructions as to when I should move forward. I had a thorn in my flesh and each day when I opened my eyes, it would remind me that it was there. However, not for Suzette, she was willing to do whatever it took to help me forget or better yet, she helped me to move beyond that thorn, a child to call my own. We got married and took our vows, for better or for worst until death do us part but even those vows where short lived.

Now follow me as I try to recapture some of the memories of meeting my future bride. We had worked side by side for years doing the same profession; we were bartenders at the Jamaica Grande. During those early work years, we had a good working relationship but never an intimate one. In fact, I had not noticed her until one night at a party that was at my house and she was among the guests that were invited. She was very attractive, and her apparel was noticeable and she captured my attention. We danced together to a few songs until it was time for her to leave. I then walked her out to an awaiting taxi and we kissed good night. From there on you would have thought it would be smooth sailing but remember I am slow so my words do not flow easily, just eye contact and a big smile. But that was not the only problem I had, there was a long distance relationship that I keep reminiscing on, a disappointing relationship that I should have stayed away from and Ava had me lusting. As for Suzette, she was more aggressive towards our relationship than I was. She saw what she wanted and she was about to take it, which made my life much easier even if things where moving too fast for me. She was eager to please me, I gave her every existing opportunity, and she capitalized on them all. We became more than just co-workers, and more than just friends we were now lovers. I can remember the first time we made love, she was in no mood of holding anything back and I was a worthy recipient eagerly awaiting her next visit even as my hands became her hands because I just could not keep them off her body. I am still not sure what she did but whatever it was, she had me eating out of the palm of her hands. Our love grew stronger over the years; we were engaged to be married and we got married June 2001. Now I was no longer a bachelor, instead I was a married man. We had our good and bad moments however; our relationship was one for the records. We went from co-worker to friends, from friends to lovers, from lovers to husband and wife. Our life seemed good on the face of it; but her sacrifices were self-centered so they were never enough to make it work. However, I tell her thanks but there was always something missing, so I was always wanting. The truth is, there has always been someone else whom I had wanted to be with over the years and my prayers where finally being answered out of tragic luck. However, it was well-needed luck and who said good things cannot come out of bad things!

Relationship drama

I remember Ava wrote me a love letter. After I had read it, it warmed my heart and I held unto it. I was at her house at the time when she wrote it, so I place the letter inside my shorts pocket and went home. That same day I took off the shorts and left the house for work leaving the letter inside the pocket. While I was at work preparing my bar for service, as I would normally, I looked towards the door and I saw Suzette walking towards me. As I observed her clothing, I saw the very same shorts that I had been wearing earlier with the letter in the pocket. Suzette had a thing for my clothes and would readily wear them as she saw fit, for me that was never a concern except for this time. Each step she took towards me my heart beat faster thinking that Suzette had found the letter and my worst fear was soon to be realize. The fear of facilitating an argument between the two women that was in my life. She found the letter, she not only recognized the handwriting, but she easily put a face to it even though there was no name written. Suzette knew whose handwriting it was, beyond a shadow of a doubt, because it was a handwriting style that she was accustomed to seeing as they went to school together. I quickly got from behind the bar and walked towards her, even as I thought of ways to explain the letter that I knew that she had found in the pocket. First, I listened attentively to what she had to say and watched as the tears were running down her face. I realized now that I should have thrown the letter away as Ava had suggested. But I did not. The letter meant something to me, after Suzette read it; she realized the same. I could not stop thinking that I should have gotten rid of the letter and now it was here to haunt me like a nightmare. One thing became clear to me at that same moment; no matter how much love you had found outside of your home, never take it home! After easing her temper, she was insisting on confronting Ava, but I was successful in preventing that. I then requested the time off work and I went home with her. We talked, we quarreled, she cried and I watched and listened until she became calm as we worked out our differences and peace restored back in our home; promises made but never kept. So I went back to work later that same night. Although my body (physical form) was with Suzette, my heart was always with Ava so I found myself torn between the two women in my life. However, I kept following my heart even while my body (physical form) dragged in two different directions. I could not resist the comfort that I got from just being around Ava; I always appreciated the effort she made to ensure that I was happy. However, her pride kept getting in the way and the many times that she told me not to see her any more, stood out in my mind, that reaction made room for instability and uncertainty. I was always cautious about building our relationship because it just never seemed like it could withstand the pressure. We slowly drifted apart, but this would only be for a few years. The years passed but the memories of times well spent never forgotten, the unforgettable moments had stained our hearts and my passion still burned despite the time and space that stood between us. The marriage between Suzette and me almost lasted three years, it ended in January 2004 the day when I found myself in trouble with the law I was in jail when she moved her stuff from the home we were living. Maybe I had caused her too much pain or maybe "for better or for worse, in sickness and in health until death do us part" that was not her vow. Maybe it was until trouble start! Like I said we had our good times and our bad times and do not think for a minute that I am the saint in this relationship because I am sure she had her story to tell it is not necessarily this version. However, thanks to my lawyer who had drafted our divorce, with the assistance of the court and my signature, we are no longer married but divorced.

I know I skipped through a few years and avoided speaking about some of my previous relationships. This I did not do intentionally to forget or to avoid speaking of the many different relationships I had, but it would have defeated the purpose of this book if I should elaborate on all my relationships. I believe that it is important to note, women have their own merits. In their own way each added something to my life but the heart will not allow you to be true to all even when the body has its desires that need to fulfill. Therefore it is an unusual discovery, for me to discover that I can only give my heart to one woman although this may not be a once in a lifetime experience, when you find love you want to keep it. I have always said, love is a sacrifice and you will get from it what you are willing to give up for it whether it is attitudes or values. Never think of a relationship as a fifty-fifty partnership but instead 100% with a hope that you will receive the same because the moment you hold back, is the moment you make room for failure and no relationship ends suddenly except in the case of death.

My journey has not been any greater or lesser than any man's has in this lifetime; therefore, I have no claim on life that would exceed any other men. In fact, all I have is my story and I would like to share it. I have journeyed on many different paths in this lifetime and although I have not yet come to the end, I have enough to tell that would last for another lifetime. This is my view, if death should come knocking, I am ready to answer. I had taken the necessary steps to give some assurance of life beyond death and that is why my spiritual journey has been a significant part of my life. Therefore, my faith I seal in God through Jesus Christ because from His source I continually draw my strength.

CHAPTER SEVEN

Spiritual Journey

The debate of my spiritual journey began in 2000 when I baptized. However, I share a different view; I believe that my journey began from the very first moment of my conception or maybe even before.

The will that God gave me manifested itself through time and age, but such will was long before I had set foot into this world. God knew what He wanted when He has created each individual therefore; I was born with a purpose even if I do not understand such a purpose its God's will not mine.

In endorsing Jesus Christ as my Lord and Savior, I then baptized at the Ocho Rios Baptist Church. However, I want to take you back to the earlier years of my spiritual journey.

I grew up in a home with my grandmother who was a long-standing member in the Methodist Church, therefore every Sunday, like it or not, we participated in the worship service at the church. My mother would always make sure that we were ready and on time in order to attend Sunday school and it was a must go. Therefore, I spent most of my childhood attending the Methodist Church but it was fun. They would give out prizes for early attendance, remembering Bible verses and prizes for just being at church. It might not have been optional for me to attend church but the gifts complimented it all. In addition, for some of us at that age, we secretly made fun out of some of the elderly. We would often times find it funny when this elderly man, Brother Walsh shared his testimony. He started by saying "This morning" and he would repeat those words for about sixty seconds before reaching the subject matter. So it became a tag line or slogan because he would start that way every Sunday morning. We would anticipate his testimony and make a mockery out of it by saying, "Dic morning." We would then laugh in our own corner because we never shared the laughter with an older person. There was also Miss Sarah; she was an elderly woman who could not walk fast, so she would always arrive at church late, again there were limitations in regards to transportation. However, there were times when she would arrive at church just as it was about to finish and that we would find it entertaining as we laughed amongst ourselves. Then there was Miss Kitty, her apparel always stood out and my cousin Roger, who was good at drawing, would make drawings of her shoes, which stood out the most. He then passed his drawings around and we laughed as we found them amusing. We did not place much emphasis on the Lord because in those days church for us was all about the fun. We participated in the worship service because the elders told us to do so, because we attended church, we gained lots of knowledge. Then Grand Maw died and everything began to change, my mother could no longer find comfort in the home. I grew up attending different churches until I baptized in the Baptist Church, which is now my home of worship. There has always been a strong conviction in my heart and a firm belief in God as my source of strength, refuge and comfort; even long before, I baptized.

In fact, there would have had to been some unavoidable circumstances that stood in my way for me not to attend church. I was always eager to attend church and was always early. I would ensure that I got to church on time for Sunday school whether it would be Brother Bowen or Sister Jackson who is conducting the class. Sunday school would normally start before the actual worship service and by my own free will; I attended whenever I went to church. The reverence of God always had a place in my life and my spiritual connection was unquestionable. There are many miraculous moments in my life and I can trace them as far back as my childhood, when I would fall from the different trees or even the time when I escaped drowning in the ocean after I dove too deep and could barely hold my breath to get back to the top. Another examples are when I had fallen from a two-story building and escaped with a broken wrist, the many car accidents that I had, the broken bones in my arms and leg, the time when my left leg got chopped or even the time when I was shot at and escaped unharmed. There were many times when I would just call upon God to fix things and leave it there. Like the time after I had gone to church on a Sunday forgetting my red peas on the lit stove. As I sat in church that Sunday worshiping God, I suddenly remembered that I did not turn off the stove. Although I sat there nervous contemplating on what I should do, it was as if someone had whispered to me saying, trust God, He will fix it. So I quietly prayed and asked God to fix it because I did not intend to leave the worship service and God did it right just in time. After I prayed I sat in the worship service until it was over, I believed in my heart that God would not have let anything happen to the house although there was no one home to turn off the stove. There was! This young boy called Big John, who had easy access to the house because he would often come by the house to do chores, and often receive rewards for doing so. That Sunday God had sent him to turn off that stove. He got there right in the nick of time, just about, the time the pot began to burn; I believe that he was not just passing through but God had sent him to fix my problem. This was how Big John described the incident, I was passing by the house and I smelled something coming from the kitchen so I stopped to see what it was. After I went inside the house, I saw the flames beneath the pot with the content of the pot as black as charcoal and light smoke coming from it. I hastily turned the stove off and put the pot outside. My prayer had answered. Well, probably not in so many words but that is how I interpreted what he said. God is a good God, and when you truly trust him, He will work wonders in your life and you only need to believe.

I baptized many years after those incidents. At the time of my baptism, my whole life had fallen apart; I was so prone to accidents. My life was on an emotional, physical and financial meltdown. Everything I did turned bad so much that I thought of taking my own life. I still hold firm to that belief and even consider it as an alternate method out of a crisis. I always stayed true to my faith, so I went to visit the pastor of the Ocho Rios Baptist Church to get counseling. He barely scratched the surface of my situation and I did not find comfort in his words of advice. In fact, the objective of his advice centered on heaven and my problems were here on earth. I left his home without comfort and my problems worsened by the minute. If there were one thing that I had learned from that visit, it would be we ought to be mindful of the person circumstances and needs when we seek to address their concern or problem. We might just add to that concern or problem and make it worse by failing to address it properly.

The truth is we may have done so with good intentions. My Pastor had all good intentions, he knew his way around the Bible and I have no doubt he had good counseling skills. However, knowing what to say and saying the right thing at the right time can be a very thin line, which we all often cross. Sometimes, it is best if we try to find workable solutions rather than words that seek to comfort.

While at home contemplating my next move, I must have gone through every option available in my mind including who is to get what after I die. Nevertheless, the good thing was, I also remembered the many sermons that I had listened to and the Sunday school classes that I attended over the years. Then there it was in my thoughts lingering in my mind, like a voice whispering through the winds, saying, try Jesus! I responded on that same day. I called the pastor and I told him I wanted to baptized, he began explaining the lengthy delay that would take according to the Baptist Church tradition. I was more than ready and the few weeks that I waited seemed like a hindrance nevertheless, I waited. I baptized in 2000; my mother and sisters were there to witness this glorious moment. I had found a new hope, a new life, a life filled with possibilities, opportunity, healing and eternal promises.

The evening went well, except for my camera that would not work because it was loaded with old film and no one realized it until the proceedings were over. Therefore, they did not take any pictures so we have to rely on our memories to keep the record of the event. As I sat in church Sunday after Sunday, listening to the different speakers, I found myself with a burning desire for more of the gospel. I wanted to hear, see, know and experience more, and so I allowed my burning desire to guide me. First, I let my feelings known to the Pastor of the Baptist Church of which I was now a baptized member. He explained to me how the system of the Baptist Union worked, but for me that was not encouraging, neither was it motivating. I do accept the principles and guidelines of the Baptist Church and I have great admiration for my pastor, who bent on keeping those traditions. However, my admiration does not stop there; I do admire his commitment to the gospel and that way in which he contextualizes his messages. I decided on my own, to go out and find a theological school that would best fit my needs; determined and guided by my burning desire, I set off on my quest.

First, I journeyed to Mandeville to the Bethel Bible College, where I received a warm welcome. After I had filled out my application, they took me on a tour of the campus and I got a firsthand view of the property and the setting of the classrooms, but my spirit still did not give in despite the clean and quiet atmosphere, so my journey continued. My journey brought me outside of Montego Bay in a place called Reading, there I found Caribbean Christ for the Nation's Bible Institute (CCFNI). I'm still not sure if it was the exceptional welcome that I received or the beautiful ocean view that captivated my mind, but I was convinced from the get go. The property is an old plantation that situated on a hill, overlooking the ocean. The warm welcome I received came from a woman who spoke with an accent she was Trinidadian.

They gave me a written test because my high school records still not found, the test was marked and I was accepted. They gave me two options; whether or I want to live on campus or travel to school each day. I chose the latter because staying away from home did not seem like the perfect choice for me. I had my own car as an advantage. I eventually stayed on campus, during some of my attendance at the school. I was very excited about Bible College and consumed by the idea. So much that I resigned from my job at the Jamaica Grande, which never seemed like a good idea, but I felt the need to do so. The school had students from many different denominations and different parts of the world, even as far as South Africa just as the name suggests "Christ for the Nations."

Like everything else in life, my days at CCFNI had its own fair share of good and bad moments, for there were academic challenges. I was not amongst the brightest students and I remember walking out on an exam because I thought it was too hard. There were transportation challenges, due to one of my car accidents. I had run off the road and crashed into the nearby bushes on my way to school, the car damaged to point where I had to turn and go back home. However, my biggest challenge was financial, my money began to dry up and I was getting very little or no support from the Baptist Church which they later justified. However, despite my financial struggles I had to respond to my calling and seek more knowledge.

I remember driving home from school one day, when my car shut off suddenly and would not start up again. During the course of that day, the teacher gave us a lesson on Faith and the Supernatural. Therefore, I became energize with such teachings and testimonies. The teacher was lamenting about how God can supernaturally fix things, even as she shared her own testimony with a broken pipe, which she said, God supernaturally allowed water to flow from it. She then encouraged us to exercise our faith and reap supernatural benefits. I sat inside the car and I began to pray, I prayed that God would allow my car to start and I would be able to drive myself home. After I finished praying, I turned the key in the ignition and the car started again, so I gave God thanks and began driving. About five minutes down the road the car shut off again, I remembered now that the bible also said, "Faith without works is dead" therefore, this time I decided to check what was causing the problem. I discovered the source of the problem; I had recently purchased a faulty gas pump. The gas pump was too small for my car so it would easily over heat. The time that I had stopped to pray, gave the pump enough time for it to cool down and give me those five minutes of driving. After I had fixed the pump, I realized that there was a lesson to learn from all that, there is faith and there is foolishness. I had tried to exercise my faith on a problem, which I had the solution for, therefore my faith became my foolishness. My faith never weakens in fact; I keep on holding and staying true to my faith. My faith was strong and it led me to fasting and praying for seven days, although it felt like it was a month. During that time of fast and praying, I did not eat or drink food or water until after my fasting had ended. I remember my first taste of food like it was yesterday, I had a Nesberry and it tasted like nothing I had ever eaten before, despite the fact I had eaten it many times before. During my fasting, I could distinguish every different flavored scent coming from the kitchen and to make it even worse, by this time I was living on campus.

The school had its own calendar for adventures and assignments and the student ministry was a part of that so I was place in to a ministry to fulfill my obligation to the curriculum. I was part of a team assigned to the hospital ministry. Our responsibility was to visit the children's ward and offer prayers and counseling to the children and their parents. There were all different sorts of sickness and accident victims, but I was enthusiastic with one patient whom I would see every time I visited the hospital. It was a little boy and by guessing his age, I would say he was about four years old. What stood out about him is that, he was always lying in a crooked position and the only utterance that came from him was in the form of a groan as if he was in constant pain. Often times I would stand over him lying in his crib and pray in my heart that God would heal him. There were moments when the burden of sorrow got too heavy for my heart and I would walk out on the balcony to release it in tears. We would hold hands as we gathered around the child's crib and prayed, but for me it was just too much to see a child lying in what appeared to be in constant pain and up until the last day of our approximately six months visit, that child remained in that same position.

There were glorious moments to counter balance the sorrow, I remember the school had planned a trip to visit the Bahamas. It was an educational trip geared to enlighten our spiritual journey, but for me it was twofold because I would get to see my wife who was still working on the cruise ship, which docked at the Bahamas shipping port. However, my focus was on the enlightening church services, which was the major part of the trip. I was set and ready to go after I made my usual connections and got myself a luxurious room at the Marriott Hotel. We stayed in the Bahamas for a full week. The church services were richer than I expected. There were many different speakers from across the globe each having his or her fair share of anointing and the perfect audience. As students, we receive instructions to write a summary on each speaker as an assignment. I found those assignments easy because I recorded each sermon so I was better able to give a summary on each speaker. I was never trouble by the "reap what you sow" sermons rather I was deeply disturbed by the "sow and you will reap" sermons, which were present in almost every speaker's message. So much so, that even on this day, I have resentment for that style of preaching. It is quite clear that the church benefited from that particular style of preaching because everyone that attended gave something to the church, including me. In fact, I think I gave more than I could actually afford to give because after I gave, my wife had to come to my financial rescue. In the midst of the happy and inspiring moments, tears flowed from my eyes one night. This happened after I had listened to one of the speakers who preached on healing and deliverance. I remember I got up and walked outside of the church hall as the feeling of sadness overpowered my heart as I reflected on my own life at that particular moment. As I stood outside the tears flowed unabashedly, even as I tried to understand my own situation and circumstances in which I was living. As I cried, I thought to myself, I have a wife who loves me in spite of the thorn that is in my flesh, a child to call my own. I have a home; and I was able to pay my bills. Nevertheless, what is most important is that I found God through Jesus Christ. What was missing that caused me to be unhappy to the point of tears. Was it my desire to marry someone else? Was it my desire to have more wealth? Was it my desire to be at peace with God and to understand His ways and make them mine? Was it my desire to have a child to call my own? Those questions may have crossed my mind but of this, I am sure, if my tears should fall on this blessed day it would be for the latter question my desire for a child. The trip went smoothly and the spiritual enlightenment was beyond what words could express.

There are other glorious moments in school that I recall. One particular moment I find at the front of my mind was being at school in the middle of the regular praise and worship that held every morning before classes began. We were singing and dancing enjoying ourselves before the Lord, students and teacher's speaking in tongues, and the room filled with an amazing presence as we could feel the spirit move with a power that connected us all. As the spirit moved, I felt an awesomeness that I had never felt before and I began speaking in tongues. Then I began to prophesize as I laid my hands on one of the teachers, I could see a vision of his whole life in front of me. It felt as if I was at a place where I have never been before. I began to reveal to him the things that I saw as he nodded in conformation to what I had said, even as the things that I knew not of this man continued to be reveal to me. Everyone was amazed; they gathered around me to feast on the moment. I spoke as if I was no longer in control of my utterances and by the time I was done, I had partially lost my voice. I later rushed to the restroom to clear my throat only to realize that I was spitting blood; after I had further examination, it revealed a crack in my throat, which affected my voice. During that same day one of the students greeted me by saying, "I did not know you were a prophet" even as similar sentiments began to echo throughout the school. I am not quite sure about what might have happened that morning, all I know is it changed the way the students viewed me.

I believe that I am highly favored with the ability to interpret the scriptures once I give into it, but my weakness has always been to retain or remember scriptures chapters or verses. Although many describe my ability as a gift, for me it is simply God's way of making up for my shortfall or my inability to remember the scriptures word for word. I have come across many whom have found this ability useful, and they would oftentimes seek my interpretation on scriptures they found hard to interpret or even understand. I do believe that, the gift of interpretation comes from The Holy Spirit; therefore, without taking any credit, I must say that my open-mind approach towards life and my constant search for substance in the scriptures has helped me to respond better. I read my bible night and day for very long hours, repeating chapters just to see if I missed anything. Whenever I read something that was challenging to my mind, I would turn to the "Strong's Exhaustive Concordance of the Bible" for translation or definition. Ever since I began studying the bible and reading books that seek to interpret the Bible, I have a desire to write one of my own and although incomplete at this very moment, I have written two books, first on the Sabbath and the second on Leadership. The book that I have written on the Sabbath, deals specifically with principles that govern the first commandment as often times the rule of law casts a shadow on the principles or stipulated guidelines on any given commandment. The book that I wrote on Leadership is on the leadership style of King David, a prominent leader from the bible, a man of God's own heart. I have also written many poems with a compilation of some in a book, expressing my inner feelings, as I felt inspired to do so. Most of my inspirations to write books and poems came to me while I was still in prison, which you will read about, in the next chapter. Like I said, not to take credit from the Holy Spirit, which gives interpretation and inspiration, but my time spent in prison was not wasted or limited. I learned that God will speak to your heart when you take the time to listen and what better place than behind prison walls. In fact, you hear Him clearly, even as you look back on all your mistakes and the many times when you should have listened to the voice of God. Therefore, my spiritual journey continued even behind prison walls. I would pray earnestly day and night, searching the scriptures with my Strong Concordance at hand to give definition and without any doubt the Holy Spirit's presence to guide my interpretations. The principles of the Bible have guided my life even through the many years in prison and without God's protection; I am not sure where I would be this very day. Simply to say thanks, would not be enough for me. Thanking God is the very least I can do because He deserves much more. I remain committed and faithful even as I surrender my life to my God through Christ Jesus my Lord.

CHAPTER EIGHT

Prison

"Son! You reap what you sow, but now I know"
Quote from the poem entitled, My Mother

I do not know if it was the fruits that I picked that did not belong to me, the money and goods that I stole from the shops, the snacks from the school cafeteria, my contribution to general crimes or was it just destiny. Whatever it was, prison was waiting to receive me and I was soon to enter like any other criminal, with a stressful welcome. It was a cool Sunday morning in January, the time of winter, months of planning was about to take effect. I cannot help but say, I should have gone to church that morning, being the good Christian that I am. Instead, I had other plans for that day and they did not involve going to church. I had a job to do and the day seemed perfect. I drove out from my home after breakfast in a friend's car with the intention to pick up the crew I needed to get the job done. A member of the crew lived about one hour away so it took me some time to get everyone together before we rehearsed the operation just to make sure we were on point. The target was marked and we were armed and ready. I had gathered information about a deal that was about to go down on that day at a particular time and we were there to reap the harvest, which was an estimated five million. As the time drew near, we drove up to the location to get a head start. There I parked in a nearby car park and we began to wait for the action to begin. As we sat there, I wanted to have another look around so I got out of the car and walked toward the entrance of the property. About a minute later, I heard a loud explosion sounding like a gunshot; I turned and looked in the direction of the sound. As I looked, I saw a member of my crew holding his left breast with blood running through his fingers; the other member of the crew had shot him in the chest. I hesitated for a while because I was unsure whether I was in any present danger. In a matter of seconds, more shots fired, as they began to exchange gunshots. I immediately scan the area and I saw the people that we were there to ambush arrived, I rushed towards the injured man and the other made a run for it, I held on to the injured man and asked what went wrong, his last words were, "The boy shot mi." His weight became too heavy for me to hold, so I lowered him to the ground as he took his last breath. I removed the gun from his hand, jumped into the car, and drove away from the park. As I drove away, shots fired at the car but this time it was a security guard and a police officer that were quick on the scene. The bullets pierced the car; all over in fact, they were so close to me. I lowered my head below the window but I could feel the heat and smell the powder coming from the bullets as they passed by me. Between the bullets, my nervousness, and the fact that I was unable to see where I was going, the car crashed into the side bank of the road. I jumped out of the car. After realizing that none of the bullets hit me, I grabbed the gun and ran into the nearby bushes for cover even as more shots fired at me. While running through the bushes the thorns became roses and the rivers became dry land because nothing could hold me back. I jump barbed wire fences, as if I had been in training, still making my own pathway through the thick bushes. The thorns tore at my clothes and into my flesh, but no matter what it was, nothing could stand in my way. However, I could not compare those incidents with the frightening experience of the bullets that pierced the car and passed my face. That is what they meant when they say, "When trouble tek yuh baby clothes fit yuh" (In the time of trouble we are all capable of doing the impossible)

I was now far away from the scene of the crime and could no longer hear the sound of the bullets echoing. I do not know what had caused the shooting among my crew but whatever it was, it must have been of a serious nature. I came up on a bridge where I stopped and hid the gun. After which I began making phone calls from my cell phone. First, I called my Uncle Collin who is a Justice of the Peace (JP) and was better able to give advice to me on what to do in this matter. I explained to him what the situation was, he advised me to call the police station and notify them of the incident. My second call would be to my father because I thought he might have associates at the police station. He gave me the same advice as my Uncle Collin and gave me the number for the police station. Therefore, my third phone call would be to the police station. Before all that I thought to myself, I could walk away hoping no one had recognized me at the scene but I quickly abandoned that thought. I remembered that the car, which I was driving, belonged to a trusted friend and he might find himself in a bit of problem if I never showed myself, so I proceeded with the calls.

When I called the police station, a female officer answered the phone and gave me her name and her rank, Constable SD. That name has always stood out in my mind so I will never forget it. I gave her the details briefly, I also gave my cell phone number and where I was located, she then told me to wait for further instructions. A few minutes later, she called and told me that transportation was on the way to pick me up, so I waited. By the way, she did not mention a gun neither did I. I waited in the bushes for a few more minutes, and then a police jeep drove up alongside the road. I walked towards it and identified myself and they told me to get inside the jeep because they were here to pick me up. I sat down inside, and they took me to the station. They did not ask for a gun and I made no mention of one. As soon as I got into the station there was already a large crowd waiting to see whom it was that created this astounding act. The officers quickly rushed me inside with my head covered with a shirt. As I got inside, I was approached by three officers, Constable R, Constable W and Senior Constable W, all attached to the Criminal Investigation Branch Unit. They immediately began asking for the gun and I told them that the gun was in the bushes; they decided to take me back to retrieve it. They took me out the same way I came in, only this time they bound my hands in handcuffs. They placed me in the back of an unmarked car and drove out of the station. While we were driving, Senior Constable W became boisterous. He began to threaten my life attempting to influence the other officer to take me on a different path and kill me, but they would not agree. Immediately I began thinking to myself; what would happen if I took these officers into the bushes and gave them a gun? Then they would spin a story of just cause to kill me, saying it was a shootout. Therefore, I created a diversion to buy myself some time; I sent them on a wild goose chase. I directed them to a nearby bush at the bank were the car had crashed. I told them that the gun dropped into the bushes as I got out of the car. They bought my story and began searching the bushes. They searched for a while as I sat there contemplating my next move. Shortly after they placed me, back into the car because their search had come up empty, as if I did not know! The three officers brought me back to the station, Senior Constable W was first to get out of the car. I took the opportunity to talk to Constable R and I began telling him the exact location of the gun. Adamant, I refused to go into the bushes with Senior Constable W out of fear for my life. Constable R agreed not to take Senior Constable W so he asked Constable W to accompany him and we went into the bushes to retrieve the gun from underneath the bridge. The officers brought me back to the station; they locked me into a cell and said that I should wait further questioning. By this time, my jeans and shoes were soaked and crawling with ticks, which began biting me all over my body. My Uncle Collin and my father were quick on the scene and they became my first set of visitors. I spoke with my father and requested a change of clothes and my request granted but by this time, my state of mind was scrambled. I felt lost, confused and alone wondering what was their next move; but it was not long before I found out. They removed me from the holding area and took me into a room for further interrogations. After that was done, they placed me in a lock down cell where I would unlimited spend the next six months. It was three days after they took me to the police station when they took me from the cell and told me I was needed for further questioning, this time the questioning were done by Senior Superintendent of Police G (SSP). His line of questioning was different from the other police officers; I sensed that he was looking for a reaction not just a response. I came to this conclusion after he brought out evidence for my viewing and his tactful way of putting across his questions. Nevertheless, what I found to be strange was, the evidence that he had brought out for my viewing belonged to the other member of the crew who did the shooting and ran away. The strangest thing is that a certain informant had told me that the police officer did not catch him and I never saw him again not even until this blessed day. I must say, the SSP was very instrumental in his way of interrogation, but he soon realized that I was not giving any details. Therefore, we returned to the scene of the crime on the

SSP's request. While we were there, he asked me to describe to him what happened on the day in question. I did so to the best of my memory. He had a level of confidence in what he was doing and while the other officer attempted to place me in handcuffs, he insisted that my hands remained free. I am assuming that it was because there were no charges laid against me. A few days later, Constable R charged me with illegal possession of a firearm and ammunition, and they gave me a court date. From there onwards, jail became home and it was an uphill task. I had to sleep on the cold concrete floor with the only thing that separated my body from the floor was the clothes on my back and a few sheets of newspaper. The 4x8 cell built to accommodate one person was now the home for three and I was among the lucky ones to have such few cellmates. As the days turned into weeks, my visitors kept coming in, all with the same expression of disappointment but some had taken it a little further, with tears running down their faces. Gratefully, I was happy to see all who came to visit me even as I maintained an understanding heart as to why they were disappointed. I tried to find reasonable excuses for all who chose not to come. I thought for a while, the reasons why they refused to visit me; were they ashamed of me or maybe they were ashamed of what I had become. Then I soon realized it was not always easy to gain access to visit me and for some it was a traumatic feeling that they did not wish to experience.

There was a constant smell of human waste, high-levels of insect infestation, and the rats were never out of the feast that was always readily available on the passages of the cellblocks. There was a mandatory shower time, which started at 5am with a cut-off time at 7am, which would be for about forty inmates with this figure always changing. This was approximately 2.5 minutes per inmate and might I add the water was very cold; so it was survival of the fittest.

My day in Court

Being in jail and knowing it is your day to attend court, was like a summer holiday from law school it was one of happiest moments of an inmate's life. It was the moment when we got fresh air, see fresh faces, and drive around escorted in a police vehicle and above all the possibility of a bail offer. The possibility of a bail offer remained at the top of the list, because it was the easiest opportunity of getting out of jail and going home to a warm, comfortable bed.

I remember my first day at court as if it was yesterday; it is one of the memorable moments in my life. As I walked up the stairway to gain entrance to the courtroom, I glanced at the crowd that was standing inside the courtyard just to see if I would recognize anyone. As I looked around, I saw my father standing far off with tears running down his face, right then and there my burden shifted from the criminal charges on to burden failure and brokenness. I have never seen my father cry before and I would never imagine that he had such concern about my wellbeing; the expression of his emotion was a shock for me. After that moment, while I was inside the courtroom all I could reflect on were the tears that I saw running down my father's face.

I know I heard the judge saying something about my case being contrary. The judge pointed out that she could not understand the charges that lay against me so she remanded me in custody for a later date. I barely comprehended what the judge was saying because the picture of my father's tears dominated my brain. Before I knew it, my next court date was set and I was on my way back to jail again. Although it was my first time in court on this particular case, it was not my first time before the court. My personal experiences and observing other inmates had taught me that, going back to jail had a reverse affect, you get angry and frustrated and such anger can have diverse effect, remanded on a frequent basis can even be more frustrating, and will stir up an evil anger and I was about to prove myself right.

I remember one afternoon, after remanded (sent back) in to custody for an additional two months; they brought me back to the jail, where I was to spend my remand. As I enter the jail, the anger that was inside of me was at its maximum level, I kept thinking of another two months inside a jail without the possibility of bail and it really had my head in a frustrating and angry state. As I entered the cellblock, I saw three inmates on the passageway waiting to be place in to a cell. Upon close observation, I realized that the three inmates recently released from jail while I was still in remand. Looking at them angered me even more although I thought I was already at my maximum level of frustration and anger. They were previously in on minor charges and acquitted, however; they were back on related minor offenses. I became furious to know that they were in and out of jail to what seems to be of their own free will and I was in remand eagerly awaiting my bail offer. As the officer closed the gate behind me leaving me on the passage with the three other inmates, I did not hesitate for a minute, I just went to work. Heartlessly I started beating, kicking and boxing them one by one. I needed to release all my anger and frustration and they were the perfect entity to receive it all. When I finished with two out of the three, I called the third inmate up close to give him his beating. He hesitated out of fear, after seeing the way I had handled the first two he became terrified of me. I stepped towards him to make his journey a little shorter because it was his time to taste my anger and frustration. As I got close to him, I raised my hand with the intent to slap him in his face. He then fell to the ground and started crying out for help before I could land a single blow. The manner in which he fell made me laugh; he fell as if someone had deliberately pushed him to the ground; in fact, he fell so hard you could hear a loud bang coming from the floor when his head hit. I found it to be amusing and I started laughing. Hence, he escaped his beating after that idiotic performance.

Wicked, cruel and heartless were just some of the words you could use to describe the person that I had become during those six months in jail. That fact is, you cannot show any signs of weakness and must always be prepared to defend yourself from another inmate who just might have a chip on his shoulder.

There were court dates after court dates, remands and more remands, and the anger and frustration continued to rise. In fact, I became untouchable in a place where the heartless ruled, my word was final and for those who would choose otherwise, they paid with blood and pain. Of course, there were worthy opponents who would stand up to me and would soon realize that friendship was the only end to our rivalry.

I can remember placed in to a cell with two death row inmates, the Privy Court overturned their sentences and convictions and they got a retrial. This is how I remember it, I was placed in a cell with three other inmates, and then an officer came and removed the three inmates that were there and later brought in two different inmates, who were coming off death row, inmate B and inmate P. There were two concrete bunk beds situated above each other, I sat on the top bunk leaving the bottom bunk vacant. Inmate P entered the cell first and assumed his position on the ground still leaving the bottom bunk vacant for inmate B I presumed. Inmate B later entered the cell and said, "Big man mi ago want the top bunk." He uttered with a strong tone. I sat there quietly and ignored his every word. "Big man a yuh mi a talk to" he spoke again with an even stronger tone of voice; I removed the three star (ratchet knife) that was strapped to my body and got up off the bunk. I turned and said to him, "Take it." Inmate P immediately intervened as it was about to get bloody. Another inmate from another cell shouted out with loud voice, "A Bishop dat! Dem man deh nuh play" (His name is Bishop and he does not kid around). Therefore, inmate B settled for the bottom bunk and we later became friends. Maybe you are wondering why we became friends? Inmate B was a worthy opponent, he was an ex-soldier who committed a triple murder of which he convicted and sentenced to death. His title preceded him because there were talks about his many prison and jail battles, so much so that even some of the police officers were intimidated by his presence. Consequently, the only way both of us could reign at the same time in a small space with nowhere to run, is to be friends. Nevertheless, I was not all muscle, I had brains and my intellect was high with strong financial backing, thanks to my friends and family. It is a fact that everyone has a purpose wherever, or whatever situation we might find ourselves. As for me, I maintained a level of stability inside the jail while ensuring the jail kept clean and everyone had a meal that was adequate to his appetite. I must say I had strong support from the police officers who knew that I was not about trouble even if my anger spilled over on another inmate.

There is one thing I had learned from that particular experience, **it takes someone who is a part of the problem to find the solution**, because the solution might very well be the source of the problem. I believe that the law should be to protect the people and not the opposite. How can we feel safe when the same law that should be our safe heaven, is also our worst nightmare. Rightly said, "Without the law there would be no crime;" which I interpret as "unless there is balance in law where the law does not seek to protect one lifestyle or culture while destroying another, crime has no end."

My muscle, intellect and strong financial backing did not make my jail time any easier, in fact it got harder by the day. My case file transferred from the RM Court to the Home Circuit Court, which was appropriate for my alleged crime, but the one good thing that came out of it, was that bail was offer to me, on the 11th day of October 2004, which was every inmate's dream. I immediately took up that offer with the assistance of my uncle Carlos who was my surety for bail.

Jail is a place for reconciliation, recommitment and repentance and six months in jail was more than enough time for me. Despite my anger, frustration and heartlessness, I would still find time to quietly pray and read my bible. In the midst of my prayer, I had made a promise to God that I would make a mark to remind myself of the day when He allowed me to get out of jail and that I did. The moment I got out jail, I went to the tattoo shop. I asked that a cross be place on my arm and written above the cross; I AM THAT I AM, reminding me that God is my deliverer.

Now I was free from the physical confinement of jail, out on bail with a warm bed to sleep in, but I was not free from my troubles. I had to report at the police station three days out of every week as a condition of bail and my traveling documents were seize so my chances of leaving the country were reduce. However, the court dates would constantly remind me that my burden was heavy. I kept going to court over a one-month period before my case finally went to trial and that is when my life took another drastic turn for the worst. I was remand in custody during the trial to accommodate the arresting officer, Constable R who had other engagements and would not be able to attend court for a few weeks; this told to me by the court. Back to jail I went, this time it was a different location but by this time, my reputation preceded me and had spread everywhere throughout many different jails. I was still king on the throne, refusing to let the officers serve a cold meal when it should serve hot and putting inmates to work by giving those instructions to clean the bathroom and passage. But most of all, I was known for my harsh discipline, which often included kicking and boxing and if there was a need, blood.

The trial resumed as the Constable R was now available and ready to give his testimony but what I have never understand until this day is, why did the officer that I had trusted to retrieve the gun find it necessary to lie in court? As I recall the incident that lead up to this trial, I was very co-operative especially with Constable R, but still he lied about the way in which he acquired the gun. When he was pressed for answers by the court, he told the court that he went in search for the gun, which I did not willfully turn it over to him. He was so believable with his story, that the judge in his deliberation said, I had criminal intentions. The irony was that the other officer Constable W did not share his view; neither did Sergeant T who was also call to testify. I also find it ironic that the judge would not allow my lawyer to question Sergeant T directly.

By the way, Sergeant T was the officer that came for me in the initial stage. When it was my time to testify, I took the stand, (witness box) placed my hand on the Bible and swore to tell the truth and nothing but the truth, and I did to the best of my ability. There was another confusing aspect that I found in the judge's deliberation even as he spoke these words: "You had criminal intentions for holding on to the gun." He went on to name the specific length of time for my offenses. At first, I thought to myself, the judge did not consider the circumstances that surrounded the length of time I held onto the gun. Then that thought quickly vanish as another took its place and I asked myself. *The trial should base itself on the evidence that was before the court and not my alleged intention.* However, what was I expecting, when the average citizen never expect a fair trial. The judge looked at me and said, "Mr. Ralston Bishop I have found you guilty of illegal possession of a firearm and ammunition." I then burst out with a laugh; the lawyer quickly turned to me and said, you cannot laugh while the judge is talking. He continued in his deliberation, "I am sentencing you to serve seven years hard labor for the firearm and three years for the ammunition." Sentences are to run concurrently at the Tower Street Adult Correctional Center. I later learned that the same is also call General Penitentiary (GP). Whatever it was and wherever it was, that was the start of a new life "prison life" and I took it with a smile or at least for the moment. After I got my sentence, the officers took me back to jail where I would await transfer to the prison. I had requested some clothing, groceries, cash, reading and writing materials and all that was necessary for my new living accommodations.

Prison life

The following morning, the prison truck, arrived to pick me and several other inmates who also were sentence for various offenses during that same period. I was mentally prepared after the thought of escaping had left my mind. I was place inside the truck with another inmate in a cell about 2x4, and it was about two hour drive to get to the General Penitentiary (GP). The road was rough and the driver seemed as if he was searching for the potholes. I felt like he was driving to see how best the wheel would fit in them. He did a perfect job because we felt every bump; he never missed a single pothole. The ventilation was very poor, I could only get my nose a breath or a glance outside but it was one or the other, not both. About half way in the journey I started feeling sick, I became nauseous, dizzy and my legs became weak as if I could not stand on them. The sad thing is there was no one to tell except for the other inmates who needed assistance themselves. The driver and the other escorts locked away in the front of the truck and they could not hear, even if you screamed. Furthermore, they would not stop to open the truck not even for an emergency, if they were even aware of one. By the time, I got inside the prison I was too weak to walk, so they rushed me to the hospital, which was located inside the prison. It took about a half hour of rest with medication to regain my strength. Later they escorted me to the reception area where my bags and clothing were search. After everything was search, I was officially logged in and assigned a cell. It was during a lock down period that I had arrived, therefore, all the cells where closed except for the working inmates and they were the minority group. During this time, you could almost hear a whisper yards away due to the silence inside the prison. At first, I thought the distance of the reception room was somehow blocking out the sound. When I asked, they told me that most of the inmates were resting. I sat inside the reception area for over an hour after which I viewed one of the most astonishing pictures of my life! It is still fresh in mind on this very day. What I saw was something I could never imagine, I saw hundreds of men rushing out of cells that seemed like cages, but in fact, they were houses for the inmates. They were all moving in a way that suggested that everyone was in a hurry; it was like a busy Friday evening in downtown Kingston or more like a herd of hungry cows just released to feed in a pasture. Whatever it was, for me it was an astonishing view, one that will always live in my mind. Some of the men were partially dressed as some of them were only wearing underwear. Each inmate seemed to know how he intended to accomplish his task in what seemed to be a very short period of time. Now it was time for me to be introducing to my new home so the warder escorted me to the D-North section where I would be located. I greeted the many cheers from some of the men who thought I was famous and I assumed some must have thought I was rich, judging from the amount of luggage I was carrying. I recognized quite a few from my own hometown and my previous time spent in jail. No matter how friendly the cheers were, I quickly realized that everybody wanted to know what it is that I had to share. Immediately I recognize a trusted friend, Ricardo (aka Stama) who was quick to take my bags and pilot me through the thick crowd that was standing at the gate. I met Stama while I locked up at the Ocho Rios jail; a few months prior to my sentencing, he convicted and sentenced. That time he was always ready to protect me and follow my instructions. The level of protection that Stama offered was that of a bodyguard. He walked with me to the cell that was assign to me by the section orderly and I settled in knowing that prison would be my home for another few years to come. It was required of me to get my own bedding, and by that I mean a hammock. The main reason for this was, the size of the cell was 4x8 and by the time I was located in the cell, it already had three inmates living inside. For bedding, two inmates would sleep on the floor and any additional inmates would sleep in a hammock. This would be my first time sleeping in a hammock. The hammock was not free and the more you were willing to spend determined the level of quality hammock you would get.

There I was getting ready to sleep in the air on a hammock for the very first time. I was nervous and afraid not knowing whether the hammock was able to hold my weight, although I had much assurance even from Stama that it would, there where rumor that inmates had fallen from hammocks and got serious injuries. First, I sat on the hammock to give it a test run but I was still feeling nervous. I rolled myself a spliff from some ganja that I got along the way, just to see if it would calm my nerves. After lighting the spliff, I decided to lie down to rest from my stressful journey but no sleep was in sight and the ganja did not do much to calm my nerves either. The fear of falling was too much and the thought of living in prison started to ride my nerves. I just could not relax no matter what I tried to do. I spent my first night in prison holding onto the steel bars that the hammock was tie, which was the ventilation for the cell. Not being able to sleep, I watched the night as it passed listening to the pigeons; that seemed as restless as I was, but soon it was a new day. The sound of the prison horn and the warders banging on your gate to get a count of every inmate would be enough for us to know that it is a new day.

Soon it was time for gates to opened and for that I anxiously awaited, not another night like this I said to myself. The keys began to rattle which I think was a deliberate act to get the inmates prepared for the race to the bathroom and what a race it was. I now know why everyone was in a hurry; it was due to the lack of adequate and limited option for toilet facilities. Take for example; the section to which I was located had approximately one hundred and twenty men at any given time, with only one standing shower and three manual flush toilets. If that is not a disaster waiting to happen, I do not know what else is and to make matters worse, we only have two hours before another lock down period. Back to the race, the winner would get to use the toilet first and all who came after would have to wait in line but there were always the exceptional inmates to which the rule did not apply. There were those who came after and could not hold it in so they give preferential treatment to use the toilet on a requested emergency, and then there were those who just do not join lines for any given reason among those you will find the heartless, fearless and leaders. Then there were always those who chose to do it in their cell, which usually came with much scorn or discrimination so that; usual was the very last resort. However, whenever time this happen, it is neatly fold into newspaper, place into a plastic bag, tied and thrown out on the section where another inmate who specialized in that type of cleaning, would remove it for a very small fee. Inside the prison, this waste package is call "cargo". That was not my concern at that moment. I was still traumatizing from the journey and the experience that I had with the hammock the night before, and therefore I was very anxious to change my present situation. I informed Stama of my concern and discomfort. We explored options that were available but none of which were free, everything had a price and for the right price you could get anything.

First and foremost was a ground space, after Stama did his search one became available in another cell with a price tag. But after that deal, I then realized that prison requires quick thinking and very good negotiation skills or else you will be behind or left empty handed. The inmate who would give up his ground space was willing to do so for a small price. He had big plans and his major plan was to have me located in his location with two other inmates. By doing so, he would be able to feed from my supplies as he was serving a life sentence with no visitation. Nevertheless, I got what I wanted and he got what he wanted, so who says money can't buy happiness? I approached the deal with a happy heart and I realized that it was time to get myself acquainted with inmate rules and warder rules; that is the first rule in any prison book. Warders and prisoners will not always agree and unless the two can agree, they cannot work together. I had to learn fast, and your personal security was priority on any inmate's list. As for me, it was about getting my own security team with Stama at the head.

Being the good Christian that I am, I would regularly visit the chapel, by doing so, I get to stay in touch with God and identify myself with the Christians that were located inside the prison. This was also beneficiary to me, in the light of the other inmates, as they would often see me as a peacemaker and not the opposite and seen as a peacemaker allowed me some privileges. A few warders put greater emphasis and attention to the orderly. Orderlies were inmates who became warder's assistants who in turn got special privileges. So it was not long before I got onboard and became an orderly.

The food was occasionally good but I quickly found options around it, most of which involved money. There were chefs who would prepare a special meal at a price or you could purchase the raw food and cook it yourself. Both options were endorse by me because of the sensitivity I had towards my meals. Learning the prison lifestyle was always costly, I purchased a pot made inside the prison by inmates and a hot plate. At any given moment, you could have those taken away from you by the warders and you would have to pay another inmate to replace them. However, there were occasions when we did not have the use of a hot plate. It was either not working or taken away by warders. We would have to improvise by burning plastic for fuel to cook.

As the days turned into months, I became more acquainted with the principles and guidelines. I also acquainted with the insects and the chinks were the most annoying ones. They would crawl out during the night, bite your skin, and suck your blood making your sentence even more unbearable. The rats literally owned the yard and they were in partnership with the cats because often times you would see rat and cat sharing a piece of meat. The pigeons were there in abundance and guaranteed to awaken by them in the mornings. You could also distinguish the smell when they ended up on an inmate's dinner plate. The pigeons had a sweet savory smell when it is on the fire cooking. I must admit that although I never got around to tasting it, the scent of it was better than fried chicken.

The medical assistance was never the best and neither was it easily accessible. There is a saying that goes around inside the prison as it relates to medical assistance, they would give you the same pill for any given medical complaint. Prison like anywhere you go, has its bad days and its good days, as for me, I tend to focus on the good days but the eminence of the bad days make them hard to ignore. The appeal of my sentence was hastily dismiss therefore; I had to make myself comfortable.

Good days in prison

As I sit to write about the good days that I experienced, and when compared with prison privileges, I convinced myself to give it many thoughts. It is hard at times to pick out a good rose when it is surrounded by thorns. Therefore, rightly said, prison ain't no bed of roses, everywhere you turn something could go wrong at any given day. Then I was quick to realize that prison has done me so much good in fact, there was never a wasted moment. I still laugh when I remember the fun moments but most of all, I cherished the inspirational moments.

Prison opened my eyes to a window of inspirational writings, during that time I had written over thirty poems, few songs and two books. The books are still incomplete, some of the poems still not published and the songs I never got around to put tunes to them. I also became the president of an organization Student Expressing Truth (S.E.T). Where I created a curriculum and taught Anger Management and Introduction to Microsoft to other inmates. Nevertheless, those were great moments of inspiration through dedicated meditations and the record is there to prove it. As I think of the happy thoughts and good moments, I remembered the many different concerts with live stage shows that held inside the prison and the star performer was a popular local reggae artist Jah Cure. Being an inmate at the time Jah Cure was always readily available to perform and alongside him, would be Serrano and a list too long to mention, but overall they gave us great shows. It added to my fun-filled moments and eases the burden of the prison sentence. I remember the chapel with the many praise and worship experiences, we would sing, clap, play instruments and dance as we came together to glorify God. Although we were inmates with different levels of criminal offences and lengths of sentences, there were no barriers when it was time for church. There were days when the presence of visitors from the neighboring churches brought blessings to us and that would enhance our service in its own way. The visitors on a regular Sunday attracted a huge crowd especially when there were young females among the groups. That meant that not every inmate was there for the worship service but for the viewing of the women, that was a rare and precious commodity inside the prison. Nevertheless, church was full, I had fun, and although my blessings were yet to come, I felt blessed.

From time to time I would get my regular visit from my family and friends which was always heartwarming although there were mixed feelings that lingers in the back of my mind but it was good to see someone still care or cared enough to visit in prison. The time allotted for visitation was always short and with a wall of thick glass between us, it was almost impossible to hear each other but the view was more than enough.

There were always the exceptional moments when the physical structure that separated us from our visitors actually was remove, this would come as a privilege on family day. On this particular day, we would get to hold and kiss our visitor, but this was only twice per year and for only fifteen minutes. I recall the first time my mother visited me it was a heart-warming feeling. One of the orderly who was responsible for visitation came to notify me that my visitor had arrived, as I entered the hall I saw my mother standing, I walked over to her, greeted her with a tight hug and a big kiss as if I had not seen her in a decade. We sat and talked as the moment was only too short but it was well worth it, we end it with another hug and kiss. The preparation for that day came with much anxiety, just the very thought of knowing that you were going to make physical contact with your families or friends and for some wives and children. This thought elicited mixed reactions from many inmates and the reflection on their faces told it all. Sadly, the depression, heartache and disappointment that it left behind would last until the next visit.

Then there were the inspirational moments, the moments when I would search the scriptures and any books that were available, searching for knowledge and deeper understanding of life. I would meditate both day and night even as I received my inspirations to write. There were times when these moments became intense, so much so that I would create my own world in writing, expressing my views beyond my control and without limitations. There were moments when I felt captivated by my own thoughts and the fact that I have a gift to interpret things easily makes me marvel at my own findings. One thing is for sure, I had learned that a simple life is an easy life because to whom much given much is required.

I had received many compliments from most of the inmates who either read or listened to my poems. Often times I was ask to either recite or write a poem for someone, and for me that was encouragement. I was engulfing in my writing at times that an hour of sleep felt like too much sleep. I felt that by sleeping too long, I would be missing the pleasures of writing, and the fact that others appreciated my writings; gave me motivation.

Then there was the cell phone, illegal as it was inside the prison, it is something you do not want to live without inside the prison. Having a phone in prison is next to winning the lottery but it had its reverse effect too. Although there are moments when the cell phone would allow you to hear good things that you wanted to hear, it also allowed you to hear bad things you did not want hear. I question the reason for not making it legal inside the prison and I do it on this basis. Being in prison means you are physically lock away from the society you have grown to know and love, which means that all you have left is mind and soul. A voice by which the soul speaks and ears from which the soul hears and receives. Therefore, if that is all you have left, the cell phone is your only means of keeping that lifeline alive. By making cell phones illegal in prison I believe the lifeline of the inmates is cut off and left to die, but like the receipt that is exchanged between police and warders when you were first brought to the prison suggested *"body received"* an inmate's death would be meaningless to them. On the other side to balance out the argument, having a cell phone in prison can cause serious harm to inmates both mentally and physically. For example, when you receive a bad message it can have an adverse effect. Knowing that you are physically confined reduces your ability to respond to the needs of others, especially the ones you have come to know and love. The sad truth is it can cause death and it is debatable that the prison security may be at risk and we must bear in mind it is a secured facility. However, which is greater, the lifeline of the inmate or the security of the prison? I say you can always find ways to secure the prison but communication is the only lifeline for prisoners even with its reverse effects. As for me, my cell phone helped me regain hope and to adequately provide for myself. Hope in the sense that by talking with my family and friends I am assured of a place back in society. I was able to adequately provide for myself because I was able to communicate my own needs. Additionally, I cannot ignore the fact that prison taught me never to burn my bridges because one day I may have to cross them again and I have applied that principle to all aspects of my life.

There were moments filled with fun when I get to hear from the women in my life. Whispering in my ear words of comfort that helped me relax and often to a goodnight sleep, anxiously waiting for the next night so I could do it all over again, in a place where it matters most. As the days turned into weeks, weeks turned into months and months turned into years, I went from having women to a woman. I am glad the lady of my life had found it in her heart to forgive me and welcome me back in her life. Now you know why I am not able to understand, why cell phones are illegal inside of prisons.

Another rewarding experience for me inside prison was when I became the president of an educational and motivational organization called Student Expressing Truth (SET). This all happened during my time served at the South Camp Road Adult Correctional Center (aka Gun Court); after I was transferred from GP, after I had served over two years in that institution. Although it was a challenging task, it coupled with many entertaining moments, which in fact made my sentence seem easy. During my tenure, I had an executive body that would assist me with the preparation and planning for every social event. Among those events where football, Cricket, races, board games, etc. I was never much of an athletic person so I was not attracted to the field games but as for the board games that was right up my alley, especially the dominoes and checkers. Ironically, I have to make mention that the dominoes competition brought me home my first medal ever. During what they called Fun Day, there were many different events on the same day, this was separate and apart from the competitions that would last weeks, sometimes months and I was in charge of getting sponsorships. That was the fulfilling part of the job for me because I would get an opportunity to write and send out letters to the relevant sponsors, with the support of the warders. I had written letter after letter to many different sponsors prior to the competitions and we received much needed support from most of the sponsors. Those were good days in prison, the atmosphere filled with peace, and everyone took the time out to enjoy themselves. Therefore, prison had its good days and I had in some ways benefited from them. I was soon to realize that I can do anything if I have the right resources and time to do it. Then there were the not so favorable moments or the bad days.

Bad days in prison

Although I always tried to do my best, I cannot change the fact that we are human and that we are subject to failures. Failures are usually the down side of our lives but it is also the test of our strength, therefore it is up to that individual to turn things around. Change the negative events into something positive, one that will produce the right fruit.

When I stop to think of my bad days behind the prison walls, the first thing that comes to mind is the first day they took me inside the prison. I cannot help but remember the journey on the road, I was sick by the time I got inside the prison. Neither can I forget the astonishing view of the hundreds of men rushing out of prison cells. I can never forget how a receipt was exchange between the warder and police for my body as if I was already dead. I cannot help remembering the sound of the prison gate as it closed behind me for the first time, I can still hear the bang echoing in my ears. Confined to prison was not entirely bad, it is just that bad things happen especially when you are a prisoner, it was an expectation I had. Obviously, prison is a place where no one wants to be except the warders, who are paid to be there. Prison is like an apartment building in hell; the only difference is you have greater hope of leaving with good behavior or at the end of the sentence.

On the face of it, prison may seem like an easy life to live, with three square meals a day, a shelter, no bills to pay, no wife to obey and 24-hour security. The truth is, I would believe so myself only if I had not gone there.

There I learned what seemed to be free, actual cost more than I could afford to pay. I was among many who shared the same view. The reality is that your very existence comes with a price and the very fact that a receipt exchanged for your body, somehow indicates that you are sold to the state at the cost of crime. I believe that it is that view in a warder's mind that causes him to beat a prisoner to death or abandoned with fractured bones.

I had seen many gruesome acts committed by warders against prisoners or prisoners treated less than animals. On many different occasions, I would have to stand by and watch helplessly as warders brutally beat inmates simply because the warder wanted to exercise his power or he had a chip on his shoulder. The events are sometimes too much to remember, but allow me to recapture a few of those moments. I remember watching two inmates caught up in a fight and a knife was use to stab one of the two in the chest. I was so close to the incident that I could hear the knife punctured the air being release from the inmate's body. After the inmate received the stab in his chest, he rushes towards the gate where the warders would stand as to avoid getting another stab. The warders responded immediately to the incident and raised an alarm by blowing their whistle. They held unto the inmate that committed the act and without any questions asked, started beating the inmate and what a beating it was. By the time they were finished beating the inmate, he had to be rush to a nearby hospital. The hospital inside the prison could not handle his wounds; he had bruises all over his body and a few broken bones. That is what a lethal board baton can do in the hands of a warder. There are many incidents that were similar where inmates got at each other with weapons and warders attacked with batons. There is one particular incident that remains fresh in my mind; this was on another block across from where I was located. An inmate had used a sharpen ½ inch piece of steel about one foot long to puncture another inmate's chest. The wound was so deep and severe that for every utterance the inmate made, his blood would come pumping out of his chest as if it was a freshly drilled oil well. Incredibly, the warders were not going to allow that to stop them from creating almost the same damage to the other inmate, in fact they were always prepared. As I said, it did not take much provoking, for a warder to beat an inmate. I saw inmates being beating simply for wanting to leave their section to go to the tuck shop to buy personal items or it could be that the inmate failed to follow an instruction to fall in line while food is in the process of serving. Another example would be merely complaining while being told to comply. The most common among them all was the beating for the possession of contrabands, with ganja on the priority list. With events like those, I would conclude that warders did not possess the ability to effectively reason and negotiate, when an inmate alleged to be in breech or violation of prison rules. If this were true, it would mean that warders were not properly train to carry out their duties. I believe warders were given baskets to carry water and the only solution is to change the requirements for the hiring of warders. Raise the bar a little, and while you are at it, raise the pay a little, so that qualified people will apply for the jobs. It becomes evident to the proof "prison ain't no bed of roses." Factors like these assist an inmate in formulating thoughts of escape. So on one particular Thursday, an inmate acted upon those thoughts. I may not agree with the turn of events, but I must agree that it was a bloody Thursday.

Bloody day in prison

It's Thursday morning, it was a normal day and I was doing my regular routine. It was also my day to receive a visitor, so I was anxiously waiting. I went up to the second floor to make a phone call because the reception was typically better there. They had a device to jam cell phone signals, which I believe had a mental effect on the inmate's behavior. I was at the location for a while, when I heard a loud explosion. I rushed from my location to see what had caused it. I know a prison craft (scam) when I see or hear one but this was no craft, it was the real deal but unfortunately, for them it turned out bad. What I say from here on was what I saw. Inmates' faces where all turned in one direction, it is as if everyone had heard the explosion and was as curious as I was. I walked closer towards the direction of the sound and the other inmates were drifting in the same direction. Seconds later more explosions heard, only this time I am sure that it was gunshot firing underneath the arch, which is the main entrance and exit for the prison. I climbed on the rail that was on the balcony to get a better view of what was happening. What I saw remains fresh in my mind. First, I saw a warder rushing from inside the armory that made up part of the arch, taking cover behind the wall while holding onto a gun. There were more gunshots as if it was a heated gun exchange, a minutes later two warders pulled an inmate by the leg from underneath the arch out in the open. The inmate's chest covered in blood, with the rest of his body partially moving. As they lay him on the ground, he began raising his hands as if he was begging for his life. The warder that was already outside stood over the inmate pointed his gun at the body and after that, more gunshots. The inmate's body bounced almost six inches off the ground before it came to a sudden stop. Shortly thereafter, more warders' came rushing from underneath the arch with guns in different sizes and shapes, and they began shooting at any moving target that did not wear a uniform. That was enough for me to go inside my cell, which was the safest place for an inmate at a time like this.

I ran down the stairs, quickly gather some drinking water and back to my cell. As I made my way towards my cell, the prison became chaotic, with prisoners and warders running for cover. Echoes of screams and loud gunshots were coming from all over the prison. The prison horn was on and it was as if no one was available to turn it off back. Unbelievably, there were those who dared to stand and put up a fight and it was warders against prisoners but the winners already chosen. By this time, the inmates began throwing anything they could find at the warders. I was reading a book in my cell it was not my fight.

What I record from here on is what I heard from other inmates who were directly involved either by choice or force. Leading up to that incident, a gun thrown over the wall and a plan formulated for escape. A few of the other inmates were aware of the plan and were prepared for the event but the plan backfired and it was the beginning of a prisoner's worst nightmare. The first gunshot was a bullet from a warder's gun, which was quick on draw as the prisoner attempted to make his escape. The inmate began firing back and it was a heated gun battle even as more warders joined in the shootout. The inmate receives a shot with a bullet and a warder receives a shot with a bullet. There is speculation whether or not it was the inmate attempting to escape or a warder, who actually shoot the warder, who later died. There was no speculation surrounding the prisoner because one of the warders had very good aim.

As the warder began to gain some stability inside the prison, it was not done without some spilt blood. There were loud cries coming from inside the prison and the word murder continued to echo in my ears as it was the predominant choice of words. As for the warders, it was a field day and beatings were the main activity. The word quickly spread around that a warder receive a shot, but never mind the inmate who suffered the same fate. Had he asked for it, or he had no choice under the wicked governance of the correctional system? The warders were angry and no matter who you were as a person, wherever you were within the prison walls, as long as you were an inmate; you were likely to be either shot or beaten. By the time the smoke cleared, there were inmates nursing gunshot wounds, broken bones and fractured skulls. After the warders had brought calm to the prison, they began removing suspected prisoners from their cells and those they did not beat to death, narrowly escaped. Dreadfully, all of that was just the foundation for what was to come next and our misery was high. The warders began enforcing all of the rules that were in the book and rewriting some as they went along, just to make us uncomfortable. Now back to what I witnessed.

The next day each warder came out with at least three batons and they were in a no nonsense mood. They removed every luxury item from each cell and by that I mean blankets, beds, hammocks, and radios big or small, TVs, pots, hotplates and for the cells that had light they would have to sleep in darkness. They removed just about anything that would make us comfortable. Still not satisfied, they began to restrict movements and the regular time that allotted to inmates for recreation became a figment of our imagination. They gave us three days out of the week to shower with one meal following the next in very short order. Then it was further reduce to the length of time we had to shower and you dare not stay longer than your one minute because failure to comply would result in a beating.

I was sickened when I saw an elderly man tooth fall to the ground after he receive a hit inside his mouth by a warder's baton simply because he was taking a shower. The man looked to be in his 70's. The food went from a disaster to disastrous, in fact, it was like eating a dietary meal only this time the main course was stress. One thing was for sure we got our three square meals but they were in line with each other as if it was a three-course meal.

By now, I know you are wondering what type of beating I received. Fortunately, for me I only got one stroke across my back from a whip not a baton. A few days after the turn of events, the prison was still hostile and the mood of the warders had not changed, only their method for punishment. The warders came out in their numbers as they normally would; only this time they targeted the section to which I was located. They called every inmate from his cell and instructed us to take things needed for a shower and our piss gyal (bucket used to pass waste matters). We complied but like sheep, we followed with no questions. They were taking us from the front of the prison to the back of the prison about a five-minute walk just to take a shower. While we passed many different shower areas, including the one we left in our section, which would have been much easier for us to use. Murmurs of relocation heard among the inmates but I quickly rubbish that thought, because in my mind it would be rather difficult for the warders to relocate 120 inmates with one move. Therefore, the suspense grew as we journey along the way. Suddenly a thought rushed through my mind after I saw a group of warders holding to either a baton or whip; I thought that was going to our day to receive beaten, I did not taught wrong. We were soon to learn the reason behind their actions, and we had two options remain in your cell and stay dirty with the strong possibility of a beating regardless, or follow and get a shower with the strong possibility of a beating. Like I had said before, warder's reasons usually entailed a beating and this one was no different. Therefore we were given orders to march in single file towards the bath area and we did as we were told, trying not to create any further tension. While we marched, I noticed that all the other sections closed and we were the only inmates walking inside the prison.

Another thing I noticed was that all the warders strategically positioned themselves on either side of the walkway and they were not there as fencing or protection for us. We had to walk in the middle making us easy targets and that is when I got my stroke across my back. There was a tall warder standing on the left side of the walkway and he stretched out his strap at any inmate who was not moving fast enough, that is when I became a victim. As I hurried in line, the inmate that was walking before me stumbled because of the slippers that he was wearing. By the time I stop to help him, the strap was already across my back, therefore, I did not hesitate; I pushed on a little faster to avoid the second blow. The fun was far from over for the warders and by the time, we got to the showers, there were warders present at every shower stall, standing on anything that they could find. They were unified in their intention, which was to make our shower as short as possible. They would literally count us off as if we were in a wrestling match. Whether or not you were done with the water, they would turn it off and call for the next inmate to do it all over again. For those inmates who thought they had time to wash their hair ended up with soap in their eyes. The journey back to the section was almost the same, the only difference I escaped the strap. Fortunately, this was our first and last visit in such a manner to the back of the prison.

The intensity of the prison remained the same, days going into weeks then months. The authorities erected more fencing inside a place where there was nowhere to run. The penalties remained the same, but the restrictions changed by the day. It became a successful weight loss program. Inmates that probably weighed 150lbs or 68kg drop to a weight of about 120lbs or 54kg over a one-week period. This may be my estimation but I have no doubt that the stress level had risen to a record high inside the prison, which was major contributing factor to the weight loss program. After a few weeks had passed, there was a total shut down of the limited rehabilitation programs that were inside the prison and a few minutes of sunlight had taken its place. We spent over twenty hours each day in our cells with nothing to do except sleep or talk with each other. The prison became filthy and the smell was unbearable, there was human waste tied into plastic bags (cargo) all over the balconies and corridors and even with good intentions to have it cleaned, the warders would not allow it. There were times when I could hardly tell the night from the day and staring at the high prison walls did nothing to change that. In fact, many inmates stared at the high walls until they very nearly went insane. Miraculous, my savior came to my rescue; I was in my cell one day when I heard my name called out by a warder. I responded and they took me from my cell to attend court in St Ann. Going back to jail and out of penitentiary was one of the best things that could have happened to me given the current situation and my savior was a police officer who was waiting to escort me back to jail to wait my court date. I stayed in jail in St Ann for a few months as the case required and by the time I got back to the prison, the smoke had cleared but the weight loss program had reaped its success and the newly erected fences were going nowhere. It was a glorious day when warders and inmates could laugh at a joke or reason without a beating. I must admit that inmates were never the easiest task given to warders, but who is to blame? On the face of it, it would seem like criminals as we were often call, should shoulder the blame for their own actions, but in most cases I beg to disagree. I could simply say if there were no law, there would not be any crime. Anarchy is never a good thing and the results of such always ended with chaos. I have great respect for the law and what it represents, which is stability and security in the form of good governance. Nevertheless, all whom received mandate to enforce the law must do so with tact and remain mindful of the reasons behind every violation of the law. The fact is whatever side of the law you stand; we are all human beings who are often times driven by our own desires, needs and bitter emotions. All of this can drive us to failures, which could also lead us to act outside the confinement of the law. Even so, there are times when the rule of law is questionable, when it seeks to protect one's lifestyle at the expense of destroying another's lifestyle.

I had never seen myself as someone that is immune to the disobedience of the law and my record will show that is a fact. I admit that I have broken many of the laws of the land and it caused me more than I could ever afford, however the laws or rules of the prison were not much different but much harder to break. Where there is a will, there is always a way and that saying applies to all factors in life.

I became one of the prison's drugs cartel controlling a large market share of the prisoner's supplies, made easy by having the right connections and financial influence. The details of any such transaction may be sensitive to the operation of the prisons; therefore, I will not attempt to share any such details if I had any. This may have diverse effect on the inmates that leave behind the prison walls. Nevertheless, every crime has its bad day and distributing drugs was no different. I can remember receiving a few kg of ganja after I had closed a very good deal; the parcels delivered to my right hand man Stama because he was responsible for redistribution and storage. My only physical involvement was to examine the product to see if I was getting what I had ordered and Stama was in charge for the storage of the stashed ganja parcels inside what we called "trappy" which was the usual safe place, only this time thieves had broken in to the trappy. An investigation carried out and the culprits revealed, however; it resulted in a conflict among my crew. It was brought to my attention to resolve the matter because it was very complex, and ultimately the final decision was on my shoulders. Most of my crew was already armed with any kind of weapon they could put their hands on and they were ready to create some serious injury to the culprits. However, they were divided on more issues than just the ganja that was stolen; they had community and political outstanding issues from before they got to prison. Therefore this theft created a window of opportunity for them to settle their score and from how I viewed the situation, it seemed like it was going to be a very bloody resolution. I was resolved not to allow this to happen under my watch, so I became the mediator despite the fact that I had suffered a loss. I told each inmate that was armed to put away his weapon because I was no longer interested in my loss, which was the ganja. That did not go down well with them and they murmured among themselves, seeing that I am the boss no one wants to go against my ruling. I overheard one particular utterance; as he was disgruntled when he said, "That is why I don't like boss." He then walked away. They were displeased over my decision because they would rather settle their differences violently. Fortunately, there was no fight so everybody went back to his own locations.

That was not my only confrontations with other inmates, in fact, it is almost impossible to spend over four years in prison and not have any. It was no different for me; therefore, the confrontations that I faced were similar to the everyday conflicts that take place inside the prison. These could simply be catching water at the pipe, taking a shower, an insult that could not be over looked or the showings of strength and/or leadership. The things that are easily overlooked outside the prison, were the ones that was more likely to causes confrontations inside the prison. Although I find it hard at times to remember all the details of my confrontations, one thing is for sure, prison brought out the king of beasts that was in me and if it were not for my mental and spiritual ability to resist that beast, I would have remained that beast. When you witness an inmate beaten by warders or slapped in the face simply for the way he dresses, making the wrong utterances or failing to fall in line when the food is in the process of serving you cannot help but to be bitter on the inside. Even more so, when you witness an inmate stabbed by another inmate for things as menial who should shower first, a small piece of cigarette or ganja, or even his own political views you cannot help but wonder if you are the next in line. If you were wondering why it is necessary to bring out the beast my answer would be simple, it is unavoidable. Inside the prison, there is always a high alert and ones consciousness of security, which drives you to be proactive in order to safeguard your own life and wellbeing.

There are so many things that I can say about prison confrontations, my bad days and general views of what goes on behind the prison walls. In order for me to do so, I would have to write, a book entitled *My Life inside Prison* because this book cannot contain so much detail. So let us just say I still have a story left untold.

The greatest day in prison - the release day

There is nothing more important to a prisoner than his\her release date and I found myself in that category, hence it became my greatest day in prison. My greatest day was 20 February 2009; this was a glorious day for me. I was locked away for almost five years being transferred from one prison to the next and it was now my final day. My head was like peak hours in traffic with horns blowing all around; you could read my anxiety in every expression on my face. I began to outline the things I wanted to do first. Even as I began the preparation to face a world that is old but had become new. It is customary in prison that once you are going to be release on a particular day, they allowed you to get out of your cell among the first set of inmates and I was more than ready I was prepared. The parole board had responded to my application for a parole and had granted me an early release from prison although I had a few more months before my sentence ended. But a day out of prison is like a year out in the free world. I had called my brother Junior in preparation for my transportation. My bags were packed and I relinquished myself from all ties I had inside the prison. I was the President of the organization S.E.T inside the prison so I had to assign someone to take the position. There is a saying that inside the prison that if you eat the prison food on your day of leaving, you are bound to come back. I was not about to test that because I did not touch a single bite of food that the prison provided. My stomach already filled with anxiety and happiness. Being the usual kind-hearted person that I am, I shared among the inmates all I had. I also had some football jerseys that I had requested from one of my sponsors that had just arrived so I was able to distribute those among my football team and that felt great. The morning slowly drifted away, as they waited for further instructions for my permission to leave. The joy that overflowed my heart and my smile lit up my face when I finally got permission to leave the prison. As I walked through the gate saying my very last goodbyes, I was greeted by my brother who was there waiting for me. I felt joyful in my heart seeing my brother for the first time over the past three years. I know I was hungry but I was in no mood to stop for food so I purchased a pack of mixed fruits at the gas station where we stopped to buy gas. I had people to see and places to go and nothing was about to stand in my way because I was a free man. My brother drove carefully on the way and as we entered Ocho Rios there, one thing that was on the top of my mind, which was to see my mother. When we arrived at my mother's house, she was not expecting me and I could see the tears beneath her smiles even as I embraced and kissed her. The joy to see my sisters and nieces was overwhelming and everyone's faces filled with smiles. Then I journeyed to visit my best friend Clayton (aka Blacks) and he was as surprised as everyone else to see me. I had only shared my release date with my brother because he was in charge of transportation. I was not about to waste much time on the road for my next stop would be with the lady of my life! She opened the door to my brother's knocking, and then she melted right there in front of me when I walked through the door. My brother discretely left us. We were reunited and it felt so good.

I could easily tell you how excited I was to see her again; or the emotion that I felt as we threw ourselves at each other. We created a world all our own right then and there. The bedroom was like a sauna penetrating heat into our bodies as we dripped sweat uncontrollably. The Queen Size bed became too small for the both of us, so we had to take it to the floor. She relaxed in my arms as I gazed in her eyes. I could tell you more; however, by now I know you have gotten the picture. What matters most is that I loved her even more than I ever loved her before.

The gates of prison shut permanently behind me. If the only way the gates were to reopen based on my return, I can assure you that they would remained closed for all eternity. I thank all those whom had taken the time to endure a very stressful ordeal to visit me while incarcerated. Please forgive me for allowing you to face such an ordeal, it is sad that my father never chose to visit but I am sure he had his own personal reasons. There are many others who I would have hope to see during my years, but I hold no malice against them for not visiting, after all, it was a stressful ordeal. Those are moments I would never forget but never want to relive. Again I say I know I am not a fast learner but what I learned stayed with me and I have now learned to humble myself and be satisfied with the little that I have and walk away from trouble at all cost. I know I can never rewrite my past but I sure can write my future. And of this I am certain despite the lessons learned and the experiences gained, I do not intend to relive my past. What is done is done, but for sure, I will never have to do it again. I used my mistakes as my guideline; and washed my hands from all the wrongs that I did to prepare for a brighter future.

This poem is entitled "How do you see me?" listed among the many poems that I wrote.

How do you see me?
Be true to yourself be true to me
Am I a strong man or am I a weak man?
Be true to yourself, be true to me
How do you really see me?
Judged me compare me love me hate me
Just be true to yourself, be true to me

How do you see me?
Stop! Think! Am I who I say I am?
Or am I pretending to be the one?
Be true to yourself be true to me
Am I really in your dreams?
Or am I just wishing, it seems
Am I of the past a moment that never lasted?
Be true to yourself be true to me
My days would be so much brighter if I
could believe that I am from the future
The future where we will always be together
But to you does it matter?
Be true to yourself be true to me
How do you see me?

CHAPTER NINE

How do you see me?

A friend once sent me a text message and wrote, "**Who are you?**" This was someone whom I had known for over 15 years and she captivated by my poems after she had read them. I found it strange at first that she would ask a question like that but what I found to be really strange was that I could not find an answer to her question. The truth is I still do not have a precise answer. I have contemplated the question; I asked. **Am I that baby boy with a single parent who grew up in Parry Town?**

I walked around without shoes on my feet, holes in my pants, if I wore any and seldom a shirt to cover my back. I tried my best at all times to add to the little that my mother had to offer, which most of the time it was not much. A few crackers and some bush tea for breakfast, lunch was for school days and dinner would range from turn-cornmeal or chicken back with ground provision. (Yam, coco, banana) However, there were exceptional days, but they were rare. These extraordinary occasions happened, when a relative send us barrels from overseas stocked with food and clothing, most times the relative sent to us clothing that they themselves probably did not want. However, between my mother's willingness to share with neighbors and our six hungry mouths that needed to eat, one barrel every few years was never enough. Nevertheless, I always held my end of the deal by doing my chores, which often consisted of the catching of water from the river or the fetching of the firewood from the bushes. Moreover, in the middle of all that, I would still find time for harvesting what I did not plant or reap what I did not sow; which is usually my neighbor's fruits, the same fruits that I had grown to love. My questions continue; **Am I that little boy who would take from the shops that which I did not receive freely?**

Many times, I entered shops in my community and took from their shelves or cash draws, although I took only what I needed, it just did not feel right. And anything I had to hide from my mother, I was never proud of such. The little boy grew up and the attitude grew with him therefore the question still lingers in my mind. **Am I that youth who made large withdrawals where no deposit made by him or on his behalf?** I still reminisce on the neatly packed, stockpiles of cash or how my crew would make someone tremble while being force to hand it over. The reminiscing is not one of happy thoughts that I cherish, but I cannot help remembering or even asking, is that who I really am? Neither can I help but wonder; am I loved out of fear? Is there someone looking over their shoulders? Wondering if he or she would be next to taste my wrath or bitterness. The thought of someone loving me out of fear or checking their security because of my presence, is never a comforting thought; in-fact it is very disturbing. However I accepted the notion that I had facilitate those action, and while change is a must do, I cannot apologize for the journey that brought me to this point in my life despite the heartache and pain it has caused many. And although my gambling habits were short lived, I still ponder those days with intent to do it all over again. **Am I a gambler?**

There were the days when I would bet against anything that would give me an increase on my dollar and winning was always my main objective. But it is best never to covet that which belongs to someone else or risk losing what you have earned simply to gain an increase, especially if you are depending on your earnings to satisfy a need. Work diligently, honestly and stay focus, and you will be amazed of the kind success you can achieve. **Am I that man who had become a party maniac, filled with lust while recklessly abusing my manhood?** A party maniac I was indeed! Lusting after women was always on the forefront of my mind and in regards to the abuse of my manhood; I did a perfect job in fact, there is a thorn in the flesh as a reward.

The question of whether or not I was reckless maybe unanswered because I was driven and blinded by my selfish desire that; left me with a story untold. But never again will I walk blindly or behave recklessly because I now know the consequences of my actions and I have learned to think soberly, guided by good intentions.

However, driven by selfish desires can swing both ways, it can be good or bad, and it all depends on your aims and intentions. I say this because those same selfish desires led me to become a Christian. **Am I that true follower of Christ?** Well I baptized and I got married, those are examples of a Christian! But I cannot ignore my selfishness in it all. I am sure some will say being a Christian is to the benefit of God but for me I wanted something and Christianity seems like the path that could fulfill that selfish desire. Getting married was just a matter of following the right protocol as required in Christianity my objective was health and wealth. But we can't fool God or trick Him to believe that we are committed to the cause, we are only destroying ourselves and that is exactly what I did.

Nevertheless, Jesus Christ is the victor in all of my selfishness and although my selfish desires may have led me into Christianity my commitment and faith is unmovable even to this very day. However, it is the same selfish desires or reasons why this question is very eminent in my mind. So the question of "Who are you" continues. **Am I a criminal?**

According to the records of the government, this is no longer an allegation but a fact. According to all those whom tasted my bitterness this is no longer a speculation but the truth. It is my view that there are many who believe that the gates of prison should never have opened to release a person like me. In fact, the Law of Moses states that an eye for an eye but even that misinterpreted at times, as I am often misunderstood. My pain is as real as the morning of each day and no matter the type of punishment that I received or price I paid, I remain a criminal to many. No matter how long the nights may seem, the morning will come. No matter the forgiveness that I had sought, my sins are always coming back to haunt me. Moreover, my sins never seem like they ever forgiven. However, following my heart's desire does not make me selfish. After all life has blessed me with wisdom, knowledge and understanding, therefore, I must follow my own path. Finding conventional ways and means to fulfill my desires does not make me a criminal. Why must I suffer so that someone else can live wealthy and happy? Hard working I am indeed; but all I asked for was better wages. Therefore, my definition of a criminal are those whom facilitate poverty. By taking the little that another person possesses to add to your already over weight stock, does make you a criminal. Having enough to share and refusing to share is selfish. Consequently am I a criminal? I always seek to give just weight, my yea is yea and my nay is nay. I would give the very last I have to anyone that is in need of it. I forgive those who trespass against me and I pray for forgiveness from those whom I have trespassed against. I place no value on material things or make comparison to life of any sort; in fact, I am always willing to give my all for a just cause.

I urge all those who have enough to recognize first that you have enough and begin to share. Because there is only one true solution to end the problem of crime and that is when we share and see each other as equals.

It is true that I can consider myself no less than a poet or a writer because I have written and recorded poems and I have written many unpublished books. However, my visions are surrounded by pride, my inspirations are guarded by poverty, and I have experience but no balance, ability but lack support and wisdom without courage. Therefore, I ask, am I blessed with a curse? The answer to that question is still unclear to me but one thing is for certain, I can never understand the reasons for my sufferings. There are moments in my life that I dare not record in this book; in fact, there are stories untold that cannot told even on a dying man's bed.

Am I a good husband?

Earlier I mentioned that I am no different from anyone who had childhood fantasy. And having a home with a loving wife, children and prosperity was a major part of my fantasy, it is still my greatest wish. But for me it still remains a fantasy and wish. Who should I blame? I am starting with the man in the mirror; I trapped myself somewhere between my unwillingness to speak up and my bad choices in some of my women or maybe it was just one too many. However, I believe it is the later; looking back on the girls I known and respectfully done so, I had more than my fantasy and wish fulfilled. But like the greedy dog that stood on the bridge with a bone in its mouth, saw its reflection in the river. The dog thought it was a bigger bone therefore, it releases the bone that was in its mouth and jump in to the water. Only to realize that it was its own shadow, this act of stupidity and greed resulted in loss of everything. Such a story make a good comparison to my love life. Nevertheless I thank God for destiny and spirited women whom will love me even with a thorn in my flesh. Without destiny and spirited women I would spend the rest of my life searching the water for what I thought was a better life. Therefore, am I a good husband? I can say yes; only if I am not judge by faithfulness.

Am I that man without name or fame?

My life has always filled with uncertainty, whether I do well or bad the bittersweet results are still the same. The truth is I have never been that lucky one and winning eluded me. I could fairly say death has never been my concern because I am more fearful to be alive rather than to die. I cannot truly say that I am not suicidal because I had made an attempt once and the truth is I have never ruled it out as an option. The fact of the matter is, a rough task given to me at a very early age. However, I do consider myself as someone who is predictable because you can always expect of me to give good advice although I fail to give myself any. Nevertheless, my name will record in the minds of many for much more generations to come and on that note; I can say that I do have a name. My name is Ralston Garth Bishop. How do you see me is of great importance to me. Who I am is a question that I used to shy away from because there were moments when I have a lingering doubt. I have come to terms with the real me the day that I started writing this book. My life experience had molded me in to someone far greater than I had imagine, but the most important aspect of my being is that I am a child of God who stands ready to be judged. I never thought of fame as something that I would enjoy therefore I strive not for it but instead I strive to help everyone that I possibly can. This I do without stretching forth my hand seeking reward of any sorts. Despite the fact that my financial status is currently in a state of dilemma, I have learned how to balance my life with the very little that I have.

There is one thing that is certain in my life, my God always provides a way when there seems like there is no way. Now I pray as the spirit leads that, God will continue to guide me even in the path of righteousness for His namesake. I pray that He will bless my home my neighbors, friends and family's home even as I glorify His holy name Amen. I am a firm believer that prayer is the way in which we communicate with God.

However, God is spirit and we can only communicate to him by the spirit, the same spirit that is in Jesus Christ. Therefore, The Holy Spirit leads us into true prayer and not our emotions or burning desires. I have learned that if we want to be truly faithful, we must never provide ourselves with options that are sinful, or wicked or corrupt, or immoral options even if they exist. However, it is on this belief that I can fairly say I am what I am where I am but I am that I am.

REFLECTION

My greatest love of all is my God. The love I had for my mother knew no boundaries but I have regrets. I regret not giving my mother a grandchild to hold in her hands before she died and there is a sad feeling that lingers in my heart whenever I have thoughts of my mother. The truth is I wish I had done more for her during her lifetime, despite the fact that I gave her my very best. Faith has always been my weapon on the battlefield and no matter what the dilemma I am face with, I always trusted God to provide me with a solution. For all the girls I loved, Ava is chief among them she stood on top and if ever I were to name my first lady, she has met the requirements. However, I can never ignore the valuable part my friends have played in my life and my hat goes off to many. A man is as strong as his strongest friend is, so I thank God I have strong friends who are always willing to give me a helping hand. I have learned, friendship is not about who you know the longest, instead it is about who is there for you and share your vision. However, my family has always been amongst my top priorities and it remains the same even to this blessed day. I have a passion for writing, a very strong desire to get a child to call my own and I am committed to my farming. If I die on this blessed day my regrets remain the same however, I would rather be judge or criticize for whom I am rather than whom others may want me to be. I know that with my best effort in life the worse things can happen, life owes me nothing more than that which life already gave; wisdom, knowledge and understanding. I do believe that I can rise above my worst circumstances and turn them in to the greatest gift, therefore I have no weakness. If I had a choice in my burial, I would rather have my body cremated. I have lived a good life with the usual errors and I continue to do so, only this time a little less errors. Again, I have no control over my past but to re-live it is not my intention. Nevertheless, an organized mind is a discipline mind and a discipline mind is a strong mind.

MY MOTHER

Here I am a reward of my mother's pain
Her life was never the same after she gave me a name
Now let me explain about all the legacy my mother gave
Through many stress and pain
It begins the day when my father she see
Then nine months later, she gave birth to me
No drugs
No strong drink
Nutritious food she feed me
Right there and then I knew she loved me
So as a babe I came so she gave me a name
Milk I would get, as I lay on my mother's
chest to feed from her breast
As I cry she gave me more just to make sure
My bones were strong
In her eyes, I could do no wrong
And no matter how it rains or storm
In her arms, she would always keep me warm
Then I grew and knew
That six of us she bare without any fear
Her plans were seal, each day she
would prepare our meal
Although we were poor, she would always make sure
School was a must, even though we would and fuss

She taught us the rules, so that no
one could treat us like fools
But one of her children crash and die
So she cries
Cry for her pain, but she wasn't ashamed
Because the child was a saint
But life for us was never the same
I remember my mother's cooking,
that is always finger licking
I remember the run dung with the
boiled banana and dumpling
I remember the hot chocolate she
gave me on Sunday mornings
Now my mouth gets watery as I remember the
roast breadfruit with the salt fish and ackee
I remember how I use to sit in her lap
Did I tell you that she was fat and how I would
fall asleep when she carries me on her back?
A single parent was all I knew as I grew
She did not own a house but in a home we grew
She did it with pride and God by her side
She taught us how to wait and have faith
For church, we could not be late
And although of our clothes, we could not boast
But off to church we must go
She taught us equity respect and never to
forget to be thankful and not boastful
But did I tell you how I was bad
So she did not spear the rod
Because she was ashamed and sad
So across my back she would stretch
her strap, so that I would stop

And even though I was mad
I was glad because it wasn't long before
I learn how to work and earn
She taught us how to wash and cook
For that, she needed no book her hands
were the right measurement
We are the proof to her experiment
We were never too stush
For the firewood, we would have to go to the bush
For the water, we would have to go to the river
Do that or no dinner
I time to work and a time to play
That's what my mother says
Thank God for that day
Now here I am wishing, that to my
mother I should have listen
So I pray
Forgive me mama because I should have obey
When you say
Son you reap what you sow
But now I know
I love you mama this I want you to
know even if I fail to show
It is just because I am slow
Mama you are always in my heart everywhere I go
Mama thank you for being true
Thank you Mama Jan
From your son, Ralston

In this book Ralston G. Bishop now famously known as Mr RallyB discusses his empathy of poverty, a long standing culture that exists in his country and its effects on society and the world at large. A Poet and a writer, farmer and a construction worker, Christian and visionary, Ralston G. Bishop has written a book that empower the enslave minds of bad choices.

This book is consistent with his favourite quote, "the acquisition of wealth can be judge by persistence and determination. However, the unwillingness to share is selfishness and greed" and among his deep reflections he often utter, "enemies will criticise, friends will encourage, and family will advise. There will be disappointments there will be successes. There will be unfulfilled desires but the only person you need to defeat is yourself. Just be true to yourself."

Junior Bishop, brother